HIS LIGHT,
HIS POWER,
HIS PRESENCE,
HIS GLORY

BY

DR. RUSS MOYER

Unless otherwise noted, all scripture references are from the Holy Bible, King James Version, public domain. References marked NIV are from the Holy Bible, New International Version, copyright © 1973, 1978, 1984 by International Bible Society, Colorado Springs, Colorado. References marked NKJV are from The New King James Version of the Bible, copyright © 1979, 1980, 1982, by Thomas Nelson, Inc., Nashville, Tennessee. References marked NASB are from the New American Standard Bible, copyright © 1960, 1962, 1963, 1968, 1971, 1972, 1973, 1975, 1977 by the Lockman Foundation, La Habra, California.

Published by:

McDougal & Associates
18896 Greenwell Springs Road
Greenwell Springs, LA 70739
www.thepublishedword.com

McDougal & Associates is an organization dedicated to the spreading the Gospel of the Lord Jesus Christ to as many people as possible in the shortest time possible.

ISBN: 978-1-950398-02-7

Printed on demand in the U.S., the U.K. and Australia
For Worldwide Distribution

Presented To:

_____

By:

_____

On:

_____

Message:

_____

_____

_____

_____

Foreword by Pat Francis

Jesus, just before His ascension into Heaven, gave great encouragement to His disciples with the promise, *"But you shall receive power when the Holy Spirit has come upon you; and you shall be witnesses to Me in Jerusalem, and in all Judea and Samaria, and to the end of the earth"* (Acts 1:8). This triggered in them hope and passionate purpose. Their Master would leave them, but they would not be alone and hopeless. His words brought memories flooded with expectation.

The Holy Spirit also came upon Mary and filled her with glory. Jesus, Son of God, came into her womb and, for nine months, Jesus, the Savior of the world, with the power of salvation, the Light of the world to destroy darkness, the presence of God in her flesh and the Hope of Glory for the world, lived in Mary. She was a vessel of glory.

The disciples in the Upper Room, with great faith and in obedience, waited in prayer, praise and fasting … until their seeking God reached a tipping point that triggered the manifested glory of God. The Holy Spirit came, just as was promised. He came first as violent wind, and they heard the sound. Then He manifested as tongues of fire on each faithful praying disciple, and they saw Him. Then He *"came upon"* them just as He did Mary, and Jesus came into them from that moment. In this way, the mystery was revealed, *"… Christ in you, the hope of glory"* (Colossians 1:27). Those first-century believers became His vessels of glory, carrying His presence, with His light, His power and His glory. They received power and became powerful, glorious, light of the world.

Now all believers in Christ have the great privilege to become vessels of *His Light, His Power, His Presence, His Glory.*

He promised:

> *I am the light of the world. He who follows Me shall not walk in darkness, but have the LIGHT of Life.* John 8:12

This promise makes us secure that, as darkness increases in our world, we need not fear.

*But you shall receive POWER when the Holy
Spirit has come upon you ... .*   *Acts 1:8*

This promise makes us powerful, with ability and strength to complete His mission and prophetic purpose.

*And lo, I am with you always, even to the end of
the age.*   Matthew 28:20

This promise makes us secure that we always have His PRESENCE with us.

*And the GLORY which You gave Me I have
given them, that they may be one just as We are
one.*

John 17:22

This promise makes us His vessel of hope and salvation.

As you read this book, you will be inspired and empowered. You are alive for such a time as this, with the powerful purpose and destiny in Christ, as a vessel with His Light, His Presence, His Power, His Glory!

Dr. Russ serves as an apostle, prophet, and spiritual father to many Christian leaders. He is a pioneer and has participated in several moves of God. He remains ready to hear and speak the NOW Word of the Lord for the Church and world. He is respected among His peers for his gift of wisdom and accurate prophecy. I am privileged to have Dr. Russ and his wife, Pastor Mave Moyer, as my personal friends.

Pat Francis
Pat Francis Ministries
Kingdom Covenant Ministries

Dedication

I want to dedicate this book, *His Light, His Power, His Presence, His Glory*, to the Heflin Family Heritage. I have been wonderfully blessed by the legacy of this anointed family. For more than sixty years these pioneers of ministry left a deep and rich inheritance for everyone involved and have had a significant impact on the entire Body of Christ.

They carried a powerful prophetic mantle with a tremendous revelation of the Glory realm, a heart for the nations and a love for Israel. We honor these pioneers who plowed the ground and sowed the "seeds of life" in the Spirit that we have reaped.

Wallace Heflin, Sr.
Edith Heflin
Wallace Heflin, Jr.
Ruth Ward Heflin
Dr. William A. Ward

I also dedicate these pages to the entire Calvary Pentecostal Campground family and staff, particularly Pastor Jane Lowder. You have all deeply impacted and inspired Mave and me personally and all of us at Eagle Worldwide Ministries. We remain forever grateful for this divine covenant relationship and the fruit it has produced.

Acknowledgments

I would like to acknowledge the following individuals for their time and assistance in the production and publishing of *His Light, His Power, His Presence, His Glory*:

Linda Cove for her help with graphics and design.

Barbara Buis for clerical assistance and transcribing.

Miguel Simon for coordinating media and communications.

The **partners**, **friends** and **staff** of Eagle Worldwide Ministries for their prayer support and faithfulness.

A very special acknowledgement to **Harold McDougal** of McDougal & Associates for his time, energy and attention dedicated to this project. He continued to press forward and encourage me in key moments. His extensive experience in editing and working with so many ministers and authors was a true wealth of information and benefit to us. He is a pleasure to work with and brings so much to the table.

My wonderful wife **Mave** deserves so much more than a mere acknowledgement. She has walked with me, not just in this project, but through some very difficult seasons of life and ministry. A faithful partner, friend, helpmate, soulmate, wife and mother to our natural and spiritual children, she was again inspired by the Lord for the cover and title of this book. She also wrote the Preface and helped with formatting and editing. Mave, I not only acknowledge you, I love and appreciate you and thank God for you every single day. You are an awesome gift from God in this season of my life.

Endorsements for His Light, His Power, His Presence, His Glory

Dr. Russ Moyer has been my spiritual father and mentor now for about eight years. His teachings and example have demonstrated to me the importance of seeking the Lord in every situation. When we seek *His Light, His Power, His Presence, His Glory*, we receive perfect direction in every season of our life.

Dr. Robert D. Corvino, II
Pensacola, Florida

∅

Russ Moyer is one of the most rock-solid people I know, and his teachings on holding fast to the essential foundations of our faith while reaching out to God for the new things He has for us in this twenty-first century are a right-on word for our day and hour. I love working with Dr. Russ and Pastor Mave because they are so respectful of what has gotten us to this present time but also so hungry to see more in the days ahead. I heartily recommend Russ's new book *His Light, His Power, His Presence, His Glory.*

Joshua Mills
International Glory Ministries
Palm Springs, California

Dr. Russ Moyer's book, *His Light, His Power, His Presence, His Glory*, will bring you closer to God as you take time to read, ponder and study it. You cannot stand in the glory of God unless you have encountered His light, His power and His presence. This book will help us to see these four distinct characteristics of God in a new dimension.

Dr. Jane Lowder, Pastor
Calvary Pentecostal Tabernacle and Campground
Ashland, Virginia

✍

I highly recommend this book *His Light, His Power, His Presence, His Glory*.

I have had the privilege to personally know, walk through life and travel with Dr. Russ Moyer for two decades now. He is a man of great integrity and hunger in his relationship with the Lord, and his heart for the supernatural motivates him to seek the Lord for His manifest presence, power and glory. This book has been birthed out of this deep passion.

Saints, there is more. Dead, dry religion will not cut it today. We need the power of God like never before. If you are hungry and desperate for more of God, then this book will equip you, challenge you and encourage you in these perilous times. You will not be able to put it down. It will ignite in you a fresh hunger for intimacy with the Lord and a passion to reach the lost.

Pastor John Irving
The Gathering Place of All Nations
Aurora, Ontario, Canada

And they were all amazed
at the mighty power of God.
But while they wondered
every one at all things which
Jesus did he said unto his
disciples, Let these sayings
sink down into your ears.
— Luke 9:43-44

Contents

Foreword by Pat Francis 5

Preface by Mave Moyer 19

Introduction.. 23

1. The Purpose of His Power... 31

2. The Power of His Cross.. 61

3. The Power of His Resurrection....................................... 91

4. The Power of His Blood.. 98

5. The Power of His Name 108

6. The Power of His Spirit 139

7. The Power of His Word.. 150

8. The Power of Unity 160

9. The Power to Gain Wealth.. 169

10. Born in the Power... 180

11. Go in the Strength You Have...................................... 197

12. The Tribe of Hungry... 208

13. The Power to Win.. 217

Author Contact Page...228

Preface by Mave Moyer

As I ponder the things we are seeing around the "church world" today, I am acutely aware that many "believers" soundly reject any prophetic warning of any kind of trouble or coming storm. Too many are not only settling for, but are also looking for, a feel-good word. The North American church is the most make-me-feel-good gathering we have ever experienced. Motivation and sugar-coated messages are filling the air and the ears that are tuned to the flesh and not the Spirit.

I heard a siren sounding off in the distance, and I knew that we are experiencing the calm before the storm. There *is* a storm coming, and we, as believers, should be alert and ready to be the "safe place" in the midst of it. In the midst of chaos, cyclones and catastrophe, we are getting ready to see the Greatest Show on Earth—His Glory, His Presence. It will increase as the knowledge of it fills the earth through times of teaching, revelation and impartation.

There is coming an invasion of the "heavenly kind," as the Holy Spirit takes over worship services and crusades. Hearts will be overcome with the awe and wonder of God, as His manifest presence fills them to overflowing.

I saw a torch with three flames burning brightly and moving in and out, causing a one-flame effect, and I knew that God was manifesting in the generations as one. The wisdom of the old, the resources of the middle-agers and the vim and vigor of the young is Heaven's recipe for a solid and sustainable move of God. Yet many Christians are "living the life" and doing whatever is fun and makes them happy, casting aside all limits and restrictions. They need "freedom from their freedom"

We see the prevailing attitude: "Relax, God is grace. He's our Papa, and we're His kids, and He wants us to be happy and have a good time." But the Gospel is not a pattern for irresponsibility, and we will be held accountable for how we have walked it out. God always loves us, but He doesn't always love our behavior:

> *Do this, knowing the time, that it is already the hour for you to awaken from sleep; for now salvation is nearer to us than when we believed.*

Preface by Mave Moyer

The night is almost gone, and the day is near. Therefore let us lay aside the deeds of darkness and put on the armor of light. Let us behave properly as in the day, not in carousing and drunkenness, not is sexual promiscuity and sensuality, not in strife and jealousy. But put on the Lord Jesus Christ, and make no provision for the flesh in regard to its lusts.

Romans 13:11-14, NASB

A great shift has taken place, and the genuine apostolic is being reborn in the midst of much chaos and turmoil. The new wine skin is being made ready to receive the new wine. Now is the time when the Holy Spirit will consume our very beings and the House of God will shine with the light of His glory and His presence like we have only imagined. Tongues of fire will be seen, supernatural outpourings, and the suddenlies of God erupting all around.

In the midst of the darkness of these days, *His Light, His Power, His Presence, His Glory* will be the distinguishing characteristics of the remnant church arising.

Mave Moyer

Introduction

This book is the result of a word the Lord began giving me pieces of around Rosh Hashanah in 2018. He told me that 2019 would be a year of healing and hope and that became our theme for the 2019 Winter Camp meeting. On January the 3rd, the headline of *USA Today* was HOPE RISES. The story was about the town of Austin, Indiana, that had been facing many problems with drug addiction and HIV and AIDS (contracted from drug needles). A very high percentage of the population had been affected, including business people, women, mothers and people of all age groups. This had been going on for some ten years, but then, several years ago, one of the local churches started a program called Celebrate Recovery, and that program had turned things around. HOPE RISES ... It was right there in the headlines. The secular world was confirming end-time prophecy! And, in the days to come, we can expect to hear more secular people talking about things related to end-time prophecy. God is confirming His Word!

As we move down the homestretch in the days ahead, we're going to see God doing some absolutely amazing things, for we are living in an absolutely incredible time. However, we must not take our eyes off of the prize. I have noticed recently that many churches speak about the power of God, and others speak more about His presence. I believe that the two go together. We can have both the power and the presence of God.

I enjoy the power of God, and I enjoy the presence of God. His presence is His glory, the manifest presence of the living God. He manifests Himself in power, He manifests Himself in love, and He manifests Himself in reality, and He does it all according to a divine purpose and plan.

There are many ways we recognize God's power. There is, for instance, power in His cross, there is power in His resurrection, there is power in His blood, there is power in His name, there is power in His Spirit, there is power in His Word, both written and spoken, and there is power in His presence.

There is power in our declarations and proclamations. When you, His child, declare a thing, He will establish it, and when you make a prophetic declaration through the gifts of the Spirit (also part of the power of God), that declaration is made manifest and confirms His presence.

This is what the writer of the Hebrews was talking about, the power and presence of God being made manifest and made real:

> *How shall we escape, if we neglect so great salvation; which at the first began to be spoken by the Lord, and was confirmed unto us by them that heard him; God also bearing them witness, both with signs and wonders, and with divers miracles, and gifts of the Holy Ghost, according to his own will?* Hebrews 2:3-4

When we talk about revival, we're talking about the manifest presence of God becoming real to us and God doing miraculous things in our midst to change lives. He does this strategically, to accomplish His own plans and purposes.

There is also power in prayer, power manifested when you come into agreement with other believers, and you suddenly find your power increased. And, finally, there is the power to get wealth that is so important to the financing of revival. In the days to come, Kingdom wealth builders will be given vision strategies, concepts and plans to support ministries, outreaches and projects that impact, extend and advance the Kingdom of God. All of these are waiting for us in Christ Jesus.

Our God is powerful:

> *The LORD is a man of war: the LORD is his name.*
> Exodus 15:3

We need to know more about the power of our God. He is more than a conqueror, and we are more than conquerors through Him. He is a man of war, and the Lord is His name. He is doing battle for us even now, and He is the God of miracles, signs and wonders. He is the same yesterday, today and forever.

Over the years, people have come to our churches because they heard that the power of God was at work among us. If, at any point, we stop pressing in to receive the power of God, in all of its forms, people will stop coming. They come to us to taste what they cannot taste somewhere else. If we become like others, that unique aspect will be lost. Therefore, we must continue to contend for the power and the presence of God in our midst.

The enemy will always do everything he can to try to stop us from having God's power. Those who have gone before us were severely persecuted. They believed for the power when no one else was doing it. They blazed a trail for us through a Spirit-filled ministry here at home and also to the nations of the world. They paid a price to have the power of God in their lives and in their ministries. It never comes easily.

The great Katherine Kuhlman said that she died a thousand deaths to have the ministry she had, and if you and I want to serve God in the fullness of His power and of His presence, we will have to do the same. Not only is there a price to pay to live in this realm of power and presence, but we must actively contend for it, even fight for it.

Never give in to the spirit of religion that will constantly work against you. When all we have is preaching and teaching, eventually we will have nothing more than religion, even if it's in a different form. We need the power and the presence of God.

Personally, I want more of the power and the presence of God, and I'm not willing to settle for one without the other. God is looking for men and woman of faith who will contend for the fulfillment of the promises of His Word. He is not afraid or intimidated by our faith to believe for the supernatural or the gifts of the Spirit. Rather, He is moved by our faith. Our faith pleases Him.

Our ministry was birthed and built by the power and presence of God. People came to our camp, to our churches and to our special meetings to experience and encounter God. Therefore, we can never settle for less, or we will become just another church, just another religious group. Our churches were never meant to be like others, a social club or just another religious group.

It's not about good teaching, good preaching, good music, and good meetings; it's about encountering the power and presence of the living God and through that experience making sons and daughters. Let us never forget this, and let us never settle for less. Rather, let us contend for the greater works Jesus spoke of in John 14 and the greater glory that is to come.

I have had the distinct honor and privilege of sitting under and serving with four extremely powerful ministries, those who understood and operated in the glory realm. I served with Ruth Ward Heflin and Jane Lowder at Calvary Pentecostal Campground in Ashland, Virginia, where the presence of God was cultivated in praise and worship, and the revelation of the glory that resulted spread around the world.

I served with Joan Gieson, both in her own ministries of love and at Benny Hinn Ministries, where she mentored me in praying for the healing of the sick in the glory.

Introduction

I was in Pensacola, Florida for more than three years during the great move of the Spirit at the Brownsville Revival and served on the intercessory prayer team there under Lila Terhune and also in the altar prayer ministry, and I benefitted from the wonderful anointed teaching and preaching ministries of John Kilpatrick, Steve Hill, Dr. Michael Brown and Paul Wetzel. There, in that glorious and life-changing presence of God, millions of people from around the world found Christ or fell in love with Him all over again, as His glorious presence, power and love led them to repentance.

Then I met Pat Francis, who had a great revelation of *chayil*, the power of God's glory, and how tapping into His presence produces tangible results in ministry and also the realms of influence in our society, turning us into warriors and effective ministers like Gideon of old and the early disciples of Jesus. I will elaborate on this in a later chapter. Thank God that we can find it all in *His Light, His Power, His Presence, His Glory.*

Russ Moyer
The U.S. and Canada

IT'S NOT ABOUT GOOD TEACHING, GOOD PREACHING, GOOD MUSIC AND GOOD MEETINGS;
IT'S ABOUT ENCOUNTERING THE POWER AND PRESENCE OF THE LIVING GOD AND THROUGH THAT EXPERIENCE MAKING SONS AND DAUGHTERS!

Chapter 1

The Purpose of His Power

Not by might, nor by power, but by my spirit, saith the LORD *of hosts.*   Zechariah 4:6

I like what Leonard Raven Hill said: "The less power a church has the more entertainment it has. If we will do God's work in God's way in God's time with God's power, we will have God's blessing." The prophet Zechariah said it best. It is not by our power, but by His power, the power of the Spirit. Therefore you and I need that power, and we must contend for it.

Jesus preached in this power. He preached the Gospel of the Kingdom, but He preached it with power and authority. His teachings were unlike anything the scribes and Pharisees or any other teachers of His day were doing. These men were of the religious establishment, but Jesus had been sent by God Himself. Jesus said:

> *Every tree that bringeth not forth good fruit is hewn down, and cast into the fire. Wherefore by their fruits ye shall know them. Not every one that saith unto me Lord, Lord, shall enter into the kingdom of heaven; but he that doeth the will of my Father which is in heaven.*
>
> Matthew 7:19-21

Jesus was a confrontational and controversial preacher. He preached with power. He preached with authority. He preached with signs, wonders and miracles following. He cast out demons. He healed the sick. This seventh chapter of Matthew concludes:

> *And it came to pass, when Jesus had ended these sayings, the people were astonished at his doctrine: for he taught them as one having authority, and not as the scribes.*
>
> Matthew 7:28-29

No, Jesus did not preach like the members of the religious establishment of His day. He spoke as one having legitimate authority. He understood the power and authority that was given to Him, and He understood how to appropriate it. He understood how to preach the Gospel of the Kingdom and, in the process, use the power of God given to Him to make change, to cast out demons, to lay hands on the sick, to bring forth the miraculous realm in signs, wonders and miracles. And, thank God, He is the same yesterday, today and forever!

God has not changed. When Jesus left the earth, God didn't stop doing miracles. He is in the miracle business, and doing the supernatural was natural to Him. When He shows up, the supernatural happens.

What did this look like in Jesus' day? Let's take a look:

> *And they went into Capernaum; and straightway on the sabbath day he entered into the synagogue, and taught. And they were astonished at his doctrine: for he taught them as one that had authority, and not as the scribes.*
>
> Mark 1:21-22

Jesus went to the synagogue that day because that was His custom, but most of the miracles He did were *not* done in a synagogue; most of them were done out in the marketplace. He did a lot more miracles there. When He told parables, notice that those parables were marketplace oriented. I firmly believe that the next great move of the Spirit of God will not take place in a church building, even though it will happen through the Church, God's family. It will happen in the marketplace. The Church was intended as an equipping and empowering place for believers to launch from. This next great move of God will be a marketplace revival.

Look at what happened that day with Jesus:

> *And there was in their synagogue a man with an unclean spirit; and he cried out, saying, Let us alone; what have we to do with thee, thou Jesus of Nazareth? art thou come to destroy us? I know thee who thou art, the Holy One of God. And Jesus rebuked him, saying, Hold thy peace, and come out of him. And when the unclean spirit had torn him, and cried with a loud voice, he came out of him. And they were amazed, insomuch that they questioned among themselves, saying, What thing is this? what new doctrine is this? for with authority he commandeth even the unclean spirits, and they do obey him.*
>
> Mark 1:23-27

The Purpose of His Power

A big part of Jesus' ministry was deliverance, for He knew who He was, and He knew the power and authority He had. He cast out evil spirits, and we, too, are to cast them out in His name.

Next Mark recorded:

> *And immediately his fame spread abroad throughout the region round about Galilee.*
>
> Mark 1:28

Why did Jesus' fame spread so fast? Because He preached in the understanding, the power and the authority given to Him by the Father. He knew who He was and He manifested the power of that knowledge.

The book of Mark ends with these powerful words:

> *And they [the disciples] went forth, and preached every where, the Lord working with them, and confirming the word with signs following. Amen.*
>
> Mark 16:20

Paul was not one of the original disciples of Jesus, but he, too, preached with power and authority and demonstration of the Spirit. Therefor he urged other believers to be filled with the Spirit's power:

> *And it came to pass, and that, while Apollos was at Corinth, Paul having passed through the upper coasts came to Ephesus: and finding certain disciples, he said unto them, Have ye received the Holy Ghost since ye believed? And they said unto him, We have not so much as heard whether there be any Holy Ghost.*
>
> *And he said unto them, Unto what then were ye baptized?*
>
> *And they said, John's baptism.*
>
> *John verily baptized with the baptism of repentance, saying unto the people, that they should believe on him which should come after him, that is, Christ Jesus.*
>
> *When they heard this, they were baptized in the name of the Lord Jesus. And when Paul laid his hands on them, the Holy Ghost came on them; and they spoke with tongues, and prophesied.*
>
> Acts 19:1-6

It wasn't that these men were not believers; they were. However, they knew nothing about the Holy Ghost. They didn't understand His power. "There's another baptism," Paul told them, "beyond baptism in water. It's the baptism of fire and power in the Holy Spirit." They needed it then, and we need it now.

The Purpose of His Power

When they had prayed that day, the same thing that had happened when the Holy Spirit came upon the original disciples in the Upper Room in Jerusalem again happened. These men received the same expressions, or gifts, of the Spirit, speaking in other tongues and prophecy. That day the power of God was made real to them. And we need a fresh baptism of fire in the church today, a fresh baptism of the Holy Ghost and power.

Paul himself was a very learned man. In fact, he sat at the feet of one of the most respected teachers of his day. Still look at what he said:

> *And I, brethren, when I came to you, I came not with excellency of speech or of wisdom, declaring unto you the testimony of God. For I determined not to know any thing among you, save Jesus Christ, and him crucified. And I was with you in weakness, and in fear, and in much trembling. And my speech and my preaching was not with enticing words of man's wisdom, but in demonstration of the Spirit and of power: that your faith should not stand in the wisdom of men, but in the power of God.*
>
> 1 Corinthians 2:1-5

In other words, Paul hadn't come to the Corinthians as a fancy speaker or even as a great teacher. He could have done that, but he chose not to. Instead, he chose to come to them in the fear of the Lord. He came with the understanding and the demonstration of the Spirit, and that's what gets results every time.

Paul chose to walk away from the head knowledge he had been given and, instead, to go back to the simplicity of the testimony of Christ Jesus and Him crucified. There's power in your testimony. As John the Revelator said:

> *The testimony of Jesus is the spirit of prophecy.*
> Revelation 19:10

That's why we need to preach the Word of God in simplicity, but also with power and demonstration. When we do this, our faith does not stand in the wisdom of men, but in the power of God. It's the power of God that will get the job done every time.

Sometimes we get fancy teachers and preachers, and before we know it we are bowing to this one and bowing to the next one, when all we really need to do is to bow at the throne of Jesus Christ and Him crucified. The power of the living God is what we all need today.

The Purpose of His Power

If we turn to what sounds good (and I like good teaching or sound doctrine), how can we know that it's not just head knowledge? Our teachings must come from a person who maintains an intimate relationship with the Lord Jesus Christ, and to accompany it, I want to see a demonstration of the power of God. I want some confirmation from the Holy Spirit. He still confirms His Word today, as He did in early New Testament times.

What the people of our modern world do not need is for us to complicate the Gospel. Some think they need to hear things they don't understand so that they can be challenged. For my part, it is the simplicity of the things I understand that challenges me. Humility and the fear of the Lord are still valid before God in this twenty-first century. It is the simplicity of the Gospel that is its greatest strength.

When Paul spoke about the end times, he did it with great conviction. Do *you* really believe in your heart that these are the end times? Paul wrote to Timothy:

> *This know also, that in the last days perilous times shall come.* 2 Timothy 3:1

Well, perilous times are here.

Paul went on:

> For men shall be lovers of their own selves, covetous, boasters, proud, blasphemers, disobedient to parents, unthankful and unholy, without natural affection, trucebreakers, false accusers, incontinent, fierce, despisers of those that are good, traitors, heady, highminded, lovers of pleasures more than lovers of God; having a form of godliness, but denying the power thereof: from such turn away.
>
> 2 Timothy 3:2-5

Doesn't that describe life on Planet Earth today? It especially describes life in North America today.

"Without natural affection" refers to homosexuality and lesbianism, which are now rampant in our society. This "lifestyle" may be more acceptable to society as a whole now, but it's still sin in God's eyes, no matter how you present it. As sin, homosexuality is no different than any other sin. For instance, it is no worse than heterosexual sin. Sin is sin, and it's the enemy of Jesus Christ.

The sin that I have to confront in my own life is no different. Sin in any form is sin. There is not one sin that is greater, bigger or blacker than another. There are no big sins and little sins. Sin is sin.

The enemy of Jesus Christ is our enemy too, and we must see him as such. Our God is a holy God, and He expects us to live a holy life. He has given us many weapons of warfare, to enable us to overcome. If we're not doing that, then we need to learn how to appropriate what He has provided for us. He gave us the blood of Jesus Christ to purge us from every dead thing, and He gives us His Spirit to keep us clean and whole.

We must deal with dead things because if they are left unchecked they will lead to death. Proverbs teaches us:

> *There is a way which seemeth right unto a man, but the end therefore are the ways of death.* Proverbs 14:12

The power of Jesus Christ can purge you from all dead works, so we need to know that life is in the blood, and therefore the blood has power to remove sin. We need to deal with sin the way our God has taught us to deal with sin. His Word says:

If we confess our sins, he is faithful and just to forgive us our sins, and to cleanse us from all unrighteousness. 1 John 1:9

Learn to fight with the weapons of warfare that God Himself has given you. War is not just out there somewhere, in the Middle East or parts of Africa. It's right here and right now, and it's going on inside of me and inside of you. If you don't think so, then I'm afraid you're in a place called Deception. This battle is raging, and the enemy is running rampant.

When Paul sought to describe to the Thessalonian believers what the end times would be like, he began with these words:

Let no man deceive you. 2 Thessalonians 2:3

Jesus taught that deception would be so rampant in the last days that even the elect could be deceived:

For there shall arise false Christs, and false prophets, and shall shew great signs and wonders; insomuch that, if it were possible, they shall deceive the very elect. Matthew 24:24

42

The Purpose of His Power

There are people who not long ago were walking in the true Gospel of Jesus Christ, but today they are deceived. Many of them, even though they still cling to the hope of their salvation experience, are not walking in power. They are, as Paul described to Timothy, *"Having a form of godliness, but denying the power thereof"* (2 Timothy 3:5). Paul's advice to Timothy was: *"from such turn away."* What good can come from lives lived in this compromised way? These people have *"denied the power"* of God. If you are doing well today, enemies will "come out of the woodwork" and threaten you at every turn. Hold fast to your faith in God and contend for His power every single day.

These people knew that God existed, and they didn't deny His presence. What they denied was His power. We need both. They had a form of godliness, but that was clearly not enough. That's religion for you; it denies the power of God. The moment you fall into the place that you're no longer contending for God and for His power to be revealed — the power to win, the power to overcome, the power to save, the power to deliver, the power to set people free — you're stepping into a risky place of religion. You cannot afford to deny the power of God, for it is the anointing of God that breaks the yoke and sets the captive free.

We need the power. We need the power to change the lives of those around us. It happens only with the power of God and the presence of God.

"From such turn away," Paul wrote. In other words, run! Get away from this deadly influence quickly! Don't be contaminated by the spirit of religion! Religion will contend against the move of God, like no other spirit. It will contend against revival, and we need revival.

Leonard Ravenhill once said, "If there is any one reason we don't have revival it is because we are willing to live without it." We must fight for and contend for times and seasons of revival and refreshing. We need the outpouring of the love of God in our respective churches, but we also need it for our families.

Let us fight for the power of God. He hasn't run away or gone to some faraway place. As noted, He is the same yesterday, today and forever, and He is ready to show Himself strong on our behalf. We just have to keep pressing through all of the demonic warfare and oppression and all of the persecution we are experiencing on a regular basis. It is all just a manifestation of the fact that you are doing the right thing. So keep on doing it. Those who love and trust the Lord Jesus Christ can expect to suffer persecution (see 2 Timothy 3:12).

The Purpose of His Power

Paul went on:

> *For of this sort are they which creep into houses, and lead captive silly women laden with sins, led away with divers lusts, ever learning, and never able to come to the knowledge of the truth.* 2 Timothy 3:6-7

Paul was describing people who were constantly learning about God, and yet they didn't really know Him. They lacked a relationship with the Creator. They were always adding to their knowledge, but it was not the knowledge of who He was and what He was about. Knowing Him in this way requires a personal relationship. These people were *"ever learning,"* and that sounds good, so how can we criticize it? But they were never able to come to the knowledge of the truth, never really able to know more than surface knowledge about the God they talked so much about.

A little further on in that chapter, Paul talked about a battle he had personally gone through. Sometimes you and I are in the middle of a battle, and people may see us in our weakness. But when we are weak, our God is strong. Personally, I've had a couple of serious battles with stage-four cancer. My doctors told me, "Go home and put everything in order." Instead, I went home and started making appointments for ministry. I didn't make any arrangements with the undertaker. Instead, I made arrangements with the Uppertaker, Christ Jesus. I'm still fighting that battle, but glory to God, I'm feeling stronger every day and I have an all-clear from my doctors.

Get ready, for you, too, will be persecuted. You will have trials and tribulations. You will face problems. That's only natural and goes with the territory. Don't let any of it shake you. Continue to contend for the miraculous realm, the supernatural—signs, wonders and miracles.

Paul wrote:

> *But thou hast fully known my doctrine, manner of life, purpose, faith, longsuffering, charity, patience, persecutions, afflictions, which came unto me at Antioch, at Iconium, at Lystra; what persecutions I endured: but out of them all the Lord delivered me. Yea, and all that will live godly in Christ Jesus shall suffer persecution.*
> 2 Timothy 3:10-12

"You know who I am," Paul was saying, "and what I've been through." The fact that he suffered these things did not indicate that Paul was "out of the will of God," as some have believed. He was suffering persecution because he was serving God. He knew it for what it was, a battle he was in at the moment, and he knew that God was able to keep him through it. Therefore, he endured, and the Lord delivered him *"out of them all."*

Most of you who are reading this know exactly what Paul was talking about. You've had battles of your own. You've had trials, tribulations, afflictions and persecutions. Some of you have suffered at the hands of your own family members. Some have suffered with your health, some with your finances or some other such thing. An important thing to remember is this:

> *He maketh his sun to rise on the evil and on the good, and sendeth rain on the just and on the unjust.*   Matthew 5:45

What does it mean? It means that all of us will pass through tests and trials. Those who choose to follow Christ, however, will be targeted for especially severe attacks.

When I was serving the enemy (the devil), he had no reason to oppose me. I was doing his work. But, as Paul noted, "All *that will live godly in Christ Jesus shall suffer persecution.*" Expect persecution, but also expect God's power to be with you to overcome any and every trial.

When someone you know is going through a great trial or a dark season in their life, don't always jump to the conclusion that it's because they lack faith or are out of the will of God. In many instances, that will *not* be the case. If they have been pressing into God for more, this may just be an attack of the enemy to hinder them. Rather than turn from them in their time of suffering, hold them up and be a real brother or sister to them in their time of need.

This is not a time to bring condemnation, shame or embarrassment upon a fellow brother or sister. It's a time to lift them up in prayer. In some cases, they may be going through some trial in their personal life. It could be a divorce or some embarrassing situation with their finances. Whatever it is, that's the time they need your love and support the most, not your scorn.

The enemy opposes us so terribly that we are all just one step away from being in great need. Therefore, we all need the power of God, the presence of God, the love of God, the mercy of God and the grace of God in those moments, not condemnation.

It sometimes takes great grace to love each other in the midst of swirling accusations and persecutions. We need to make a point of standing firmly with our brothers and sisters. We will need their support in our own time of trial.

According to Paul, things of this nature will get *"worse and worse"*:

> *But evil men and seducers shall wax worse and worse, deceiving, and being deceived.*
>
> 2 Timothy 3:13

Keep in mind that Paul was speaking about the end times, what he called *"perilous times,"* and what believers will suffer and overcome. And what was his counsel?

> *But continue thou in the things which thou hast learned and hast been assured of, knowing of whom thou hast learned them.*
>
> 2 Timothy 3:14

So, we need to go back to the foundational truths of the Word of God, what we have been taught, and cling to it. What are the foundational truths of the Word? The power of the cross, of the blood, of the name of Jesus, of the Spirit of God, of the Word of God. Through remembering these things, we can gain power to overcome and to help others overcome.

Don't be so foolish as to think that you can do it on your own. We all need the power of God to overcome these situations. Therefore, we need to go back to our power sources, back to the Word of God that is strong in our hearts.

Originally, there were no chapter divisions in these letters to the churches. The divisions were put in there later to help us find our way around the Bible. In the next verses, Paul charges Timothy, commissions him and sets him in place, telling him to *"preach the word,"* etc.:

> *I charge thee therefore before God, and the Lord Jesus Christ, who shall judge the quick and the dead at his appearing and his kingdom; preach the word; be instant in season, out of season; reprove, rebuke, exhort with all long suffering and doctrine. For the time will come when they will not endure sound doctrine; but after their own lusts shall they heap to themselves teachers, having itching ears; and they shall turn away their ears from the truth, and shall be turned*

unto fables. But watch thou in all things, endure afflictions, do the work of an evangelist, make full proof of thy ministry.   2 Timothy 4:3-5

"Endure affliction." Paul knew it would invariably come. *"Do the work of an evangelist, and make full proof of thy ministry."* Timothy was to overcome whatever came his way through the power and presence of God and then go on to do the work God had personally assigned to him.

Many of you have had a ministry from the moment you said Yes to Jesus, and you still have a ministry. Make full proof of that ministry. Don't get caught up in the things of this world because this world will try to run you down. This world will bring you nothing but distractions. It will bring false wealth. It will bring a "success" that is only success in the mind and heart of man.

There comes a time for every one of us to make choices. Will we choose the way of the Spirit or the way of the natural? There is worldly wisdom, and there is godly wisdom, and we need to know the difference. There is God's will, and there is your own will, and the two are very different. We need to know what His purpose for us in this particular season of our life is and how we can fulfill it. There will always be "good things" for us to do, but the good can be the enemy of the great.

Often, as I was pressing into God for His best, I saw others who were doing the same. Then, suddenly, their boss called and offered them an overtime opportunity, and that "opportunity" distracted them from the fullness of what God had for them, and they lost out.

Perhaps they were pulled aside because they could not see God's blessings coming. Once we become a true believer in Jesus Christ, it is difficult for the enemy to tempt us to do drugs or alcohol, to openly steal, or to commit adultery, so he uses something subtle, something that seems "good" in itself. It may even seem like a blessing, like an answer to prayer. But, all too often, this lesser blessing robs us of God's best for our lives. The devil uses something "good" rather than something "God." And there is no scarcity of "good" things to do today. The only right thing to do is the perfect will of God for you at any given moment.

Many ministers I know could earn much more doing something else in life. Do they owe it to their families to earn as much as they can? It sounds good, but choosing to serve Christ, whatever that means, is always the right choice. Once you have discovered the will of God, don't turn back from it for any reason. Press forward into His complete will for your life.

When you know that you have done the right thing, then never look back. Keep moving forward. If God has called you, then hold on to that call. Know the gifts He has given you and the call He has placed on your life and stick with them. The enemy will try everything in his power to pull you aside. Again, he will rarely do it with something evil. He will use something that seems very good, something that can occupy your time and consume your talents, keeping you from God's best.

There is just one thing that you must do in life, and that is the "God" thing. Leave the "good" things for others to do. This demands that you know the will of God, the purpose of God and the call of God that's on your life. Then you have to stick to it, not looking to the right or to the left, but just following after God.

This is a narrow way and a straight gate, and the average person does not want to go through it. They may do the will of God as they see it, but not the perfect will of God, not the high call of God. Paul was determined to do the perfect will of God, and he encouraged Timothy to do the same.

Go after the high call of God for your life. Just any old call will not do. God had a plan for you before He laid the foundations of the Universe. Find it and put all of your time and energy into fulfilling it. There may be many doors opened to you, but only one of those doors is God's plan for your life.

Man may open other doors to you, and Satan will surely open his share of doors to you. Only God's door will take you where you really want to go. Since you don't know what is best for your life, be a good soldier, obeying the orders of the Lord of Hosts, the Lord of the Battle.

Paul admonished Timothy:

> *Thou therefore, my son, be strong in the grace that is in Christ Jesus. And the things that thou hast heard of me among many witnesses, the same commit thou to faithful men, who shall be able to teach others also. Thou therefore endure hardness, as a good soldier of Jesus Christ.*
>
> 2 Timothy 2:1-3

Timothy was Paul's spiritual son, and Paul felt responsible for him. Timothy had been well taught by his mother and grandmother and, as a young man, had acquitted himself well, gaining the respect of many in the wider Christian community. Paul, an older man, could see into Timothy's future and knew that many things would try to pull him away from his destiny, away from the power and the presence of God.

Timothy was a man *"approved by God,"* a man who despite his youth, knew how to move in the power of the Spirit. Therefore God had ordained him and anointed him, and Paul had commissioned him and was now telling him steps to take to preserve and fulfill his *"holy calling"* (2 Timothy 1:9).

Here in chapter 2, Paul tells Timothy that he must *"endure hardness."* Paul was the same man who had expressed a desire to know Christ in His sufferings. Personally I can say that some of the most wonderful times I have had in the Spirit were some of the worst times for me in the natural. When I was at some of the lowest points of my life, I had the greatest spiritual experiences of my life. Riding our high horse into town is not the way to go. We must learn to *"endure hardness as a good soldier of Christ Jesus."*

God is calling forth His army, calling forth those who will serve as His faithful soldiers.

Paul continued:

*No man that warreth entangles himself with the
affairs of this life; that he may please him who
hath chosen him to be a good soldier.*

2 Timothy 2:4

God's has called you to be an end-time warrior,
to be a soldier for the Lord. Whatever you do, don't
get entangled with worldly affairs. Be a good soldier. Come forward. Be ready to endure affliction
and hardship. Continue to go after God. Contend
for the power to overcome everything the enemy
sends against you.

Far too often, we get so entangled with the things
of this world that we choose to live a life of ease in
a land of distractions. North America is a land of
total distraction, and we need to fight distraction at
every turn because the enemy would like nothing
better than to distract us and discourage us. His
end game is to disappoint us, to cause us to be disappointed with God's expressed purpose and our
specific calling.

Disappointment, discouragement and despair are
all bedfellows. We feel disappointed, and then we
get distracted and fail to move forward. Right now,
we are in a season of tremendous battle and tremendous deception. We need discerning of spirits more

than we have ever needed it. We need to know who God is, not who God was last week, last month or last year, who He is now!

Many times, people come to me and tell me what God has called them to do. Then, just a few months later, they come with a totally different thing and are convinced that God has called them to do it. The problem is that every few months they seem to have a new calling and are starting all over again. In the meantime, nothing is getting done. Does God really change His mind that much? I don't think so.

When Peter denied Christ three times, he must have known that he would face such battles. According to Jesus, Peter just needed someone to pray for him. Tell a friend, "I'm going to pray for you. I know you will be going through a battle. Instead of criticizing you, I will pray for you."

It was a most difficult time for Peter. The disciples had all scattered, their hopes and dreams shattered by the crucifixion of their Master. Peter had said to the others, "I'm going fishing,"(see John 21:3). He didn't just mean that he was going to do some fishing to relax and get his thoughts together. He was a fisherman by trade, and what he meant was that he was going back to his old life. Still, when he told them that, the other disciples decided to join him.

Whatever you do, don't go back. Go forward. Wait on God and serve Him with all your strength and with all your might. He is worthy. He is True and Faithful. He is just, and He will never let you down. He is greater than all the silver and gold, greater than all the accolades of men. It's not about fortune, and it's not about fame. It's about serving God with all you are, all you have and all you want to be. Every single hope that is inside of you is from God. Use it for His glory!

How about it? Personally, I am more hungry today than I've ever been in my life. And I want to contend to the end, to the last possible moment. I want to fight to the death. Death, for us, is a victory. Therefore, I have a win-win situation before me, and I must press toward it.

We have the power to win, and we can't lose unless we give up and turn back. Just continue going forward and victory is assured. With all your strength with all your might, with all you have and with all you hope to be, press in to *His Light, His Power, His Presence, His Glory.*

Heavenly Father,

Send Your power and Your love. Place a hunger in our hearts for Your presence, Your Kingdom and Your righteousness. Draw us together, the tribe of Hungry, and light the fire in us again!

In Jesus' name,

Amen!

IT'S NOT ABOUT FORTUNE, AND IT'S NOT ABOUT FAME. IT'S ABOUT SERVING GOD WITH ALL YOU ARE, ALL YOU HAVE AND ALL YOU WANT TO BE!

Chapter 2

The Power of His Cross

For Christ sent me not to baptize, but to preach the gospel: … not with wisdom of words, lest the cross of Christ should be made of none effect.
1 Corinthians 1:17

Yes, there is power in His cross, and we can never forget that fact. Near the end of 2018, I had one of our brothers in Pensacola put up a beautiful old rugged cross in the church. Today's believers must understand the cross and its power. I wanted to be sure that the power of the cross was not somehow overlooked. It is far too important.

God is revealing many wonderful things to His people in these days, but in actuality, there is nothing new under the sun (as Solomon so eloquently put it in Ecclesiastes). The Scriptures are clear:

> *Jesus Christ the same yesterday, and to day, and*
> *for ever.*   Hebrews 13:8

Jesus is the same, and the power of His cross is the same.

God is giving us new songs and revealing to us things that have long been hidden, not *from* us but *for* us. He has reserved them for us and for our families, our children and grandchildren, so that we might walk in the fullness of our end-time destiny. I firmly believe that we are the generation that will usher in the second coming of Christ, and we will see end-time prophecy unfolding before our eyes. Our very declarations and proclamations release revelation and, with it, they release new power.

It is God's will that we go from one revelation to another, but sometimes in the process we forget our roots. In order for us to achieve our destiny, we must reach back and touch our roots. We must know who we are and where we have come from, and to discover that we must know the roots of who Jesus is, how He works and what He does. Our God is a God of order and structure, and we must respect that order and structure.

This fact is not restrictive. We have seen the power of God sweep in among us, and with it, a release of His gifts. In the process, people are touched and healed! But in all of that, there is an absolute divine order. It may look a bit chaotic to the natural eye, but it's not at all. When the power of God moves among us, something beautiful always happens, and it happens in divine order.

God knows exactly what He is doing, and He has established patterns, places, and things we can do to access His power. Again, this is not restricting us. God *wants* us to access that power. He *wants* for every single one of us to walk fully in His power and presence. In fact, there is a generation now being released, according to Habakkuk 2:14, that will carry the knowledge of the glory of the Lord around the world so that the whole earth is covered with that knowledge. What could be more wonderful?

Isaiah also spoke of the whole world being covered with the glory of the Lord. Habakkuk said that the world would be covered with the *knowledge* of the glory of the Lord. That means there will be an understanding of God's power and His presence because the end-time Church will need to effectively walk in that power and presence,

Therefore, we need to know the foundational truths of our faith, and we also need to know the great revelatory things that God is doing in our generation. Therefore, we must be able to hear His voice clearly, so that we can be obedient and walk out this revelation, this mandate, this prophetic destiny that the end-time Church is carrying.

It is a great honor to be part of the end-time Church. In fact, the apostle Paul now wishes that he were where we are, even though he is in the very presence of the Lord. These are the days that every prophet prophesied about and looked forward to. We are that chosen generation, and so they wish they were here right now.

Some people say they wish they had been where Paul walked and had been able to walk with him. They must not have read the Bible stories well, because things became very difficult for him at times. Some of your journey may not be easy either. Get ready for whatever comes. Your journey will surely not be a walk in the park. There will be opposition, and there will be persecution. But the greatest blessings of God come to us in the midst of persecution.

Paul had a deep longing to know Christ *"in the power of His resurrection"* (Philippians 3:10). In other words, he wanted to know Jesus alive and well. You can only know the Lord in the power of His resurrection and in His sufferings by going through some trials, tribulations and persecutions of your own.

The Power of His Cross

Whatever you are facing or will face, I want you to know that the Lord is with you. You don't have to fight your battles alone. He is more than capable of fighting them for you.

Our battles are not against flesh and blood. There are evil powers and principalities, and we must learn to fight them with spiritual weapons, not natural ones. We need to wield spiritual weapons, especially *"the sword of the Spirit, which is the word of God"* (Ephesians 6:17). This was what Jesus used to fight the devil in the wilderness and then as He continued walking the Earth. Keep that sword in one hand, and have a towel in the other, so that you can wash your brothers' feet and walk in a place of forgiveness, with a heart that is open and vulnerable.

One of the most difficult things about leading in the Body of Christ today is being able to be vulnerable again and again, after you have suffered at the hand of church political systems. Lots of bad things happen in the church, making it look like just a microcosm of the world at large. It shouldn't be that way. The people of the world are suffering from an identity crisis, but the same is true of much of the church. You and I must know who we are and what we are called to. We are people of the cross.

Know that just as you can be hurt in the day-to-day workings of life in general, you can also be hurt in the church. If you want to advance, you have to get over that hurt, and you're not really over it unless you're ready to become vulnerable again. If you have suffered in past relationships, whether in marriage or business, you will never successfully begin a new relationship until you are willing to get over the past hurts and make yourself vulnerable again.

We have all heard by now the famous saying, "Hurting people hurt other people." You first need to be healed of all your past hurts, and then you need to open your heart and become vulnerable to others again, or you will spend the rest of your life in bitterness and failure.

As leaders, we have a most difficult situation. In Proverbs 4:7, the Lord tells us to get wisdom, as it is *"the principle thing."* Later in that chapter, however, He said *"above all else,"* meaning even above wisdom, *"guard your heart"* (Proverbs 4:23). Your heart must be prepared and open to reconciliation and restoration, which is a mark of the great season we are walking through right now

Again, this end-time church must not lose touch with our foundational issues, and one of the most important of them is the power of the cross. Paul was concerned *"lest the cross of Christ should be made of none effect"* (1

Corinthians 1:17). There are things that can negate the power of God, and two of them are our traditions and our culture. They can make the Word of God *"of none effect."*

Man's wisdom does not agree with God's wisdom. Sometimes, when we are looking for wisdom, we're looking in the wrong places. There's a vast difference between worldly wisdom and spiritual wisdom.

I'm not saying that the fruit of spiritual wisdom will also make you wise in the things of this world. In fact, the Bible tells us that the world is sometimes wiser than we are about worldly matters. And that should not be. We have the gift of the word of wisdom, and we have the Spirit of wisdom within us, and that should give us natural wisdom as well as spiritual wisdom. But there is a definite difference between worldly wisdom and godly wisdom, and we need to know the difference.

Paul went on:

> *For the preaching of the cross is to them that perish foolishness; but unto us which are saved it is the power of God.*   1 Corinthians 1:18

The power of the cross, the knowledge of the cross, the understanding of the power of the cross should be of interest to each of us. The power of the cross

67

is the very power of God. Many are moving on to new revelations and leaving the cross behind, and we cannot afford to do that. The cross has a unique place in our faith and must not be abandoned.

Whatever you do, don't leave the cross behind Don't leave your faith behind. It's okay to move into a new revelation, but when you do, don't leave the foundational revelations of the faith behind. You will need those in your next season. When God gives us new revelation, He is not getting rid of something; He is bringing His truths to us in a fresh revelation, and He's building on the foundations that have already been laid.

Many of the latest revelatory words are coming from young voices, but the danger I see is that they are saying, "Go beyond the cross!" Going beyond is all well and good, but just don't leave the cross behind. It is the centerpiece of our faith. Some may be running away from the cross, but I am running toward it. It is my only hope. It is the very power of God. In it is the work of salvation that continues to operate in my life on a daily basis.

From the day I met the Lord until the day He takes me to be with Him, the cross has a major role to play in my Christian life. Yes, we want change. Yes, we want to receive more. Yes, we want to go forward. But that can never mean leaving the cross behind.

The Power of His Cross

It is only at the cross that I can find the hope I need. That's the one place I can find the forgiveness I need. The cross is the place of new life, and I need to live this new life today and tomorrow, so I cannot cast aside the cross—whatever else I do.

Not only is the cross a place of new life; it is a place of power, power that I can access:

> *For it is written, I will destroy the wisdom of the wise, and will bring to nothing the understanding of the prudent.* 1 Corinthians 1:19

That's why we can't trust in our own wisdom. As the final days come, we will need wisdom from God and His wisdom alone. It is important that we understand the power of the cross:

Look at verses 22 and 23:

> *For the Jews require a sign, and the Greeks seek after wisdom: but we preach Christ crucified, unto the Jews a stumbling block, and unto the Greeks foolishness.* 1 Corinthians 1:22-23

Foolishness? What does that mean? The Jews were the religious community of the day, and the Greeks were the scholars, the so-called "experts." For the

Jews, their tradition was stronger than the cross. And, for the Greeks, what happened on the cross made no sense at all. The cross, therefore, became a stumblingblock to the Jews and sheer foolishness to the Greeks.

When you and I were confronted with the work of the cross, the blood that Jesus shed there as a sacrifice for our sins, that defied all natural wisdom. That revelation had to be received with childlike faith. Worldly wisdom rejects such ideas.

The Greeks were considered to be the smartest people of their time. Many of them were philosophers, all about wisdom, and, to them, the cross was sheer foolishness. Is it any different today? Many of our most well-educated people cannot receive the simple truths of our salvation and the power that is in the work of the cross. That blessed cross is still a stumblingblock to many, Jews and otherwise, and it is still foolishness to many who consider themselves to be wise in this world. To you and me, the cross represents our hope, our future. It is the power of God and the wisdom of God made manifest. It may be foolishness, but it is *the foolishness of God*:

> *But unto them which are called, both Jews and Greeks, Christ the power of God, and the*

wisdom of God. Because the foolishness of God is wiser than men; and the weakness of God is stronger than men.   1 Corinthians 1:24-25

We desperately need to understand the power of spiritual wisdom.

Many of you who are reading this are called to the work of the ministry, have a heart for the apostolic and the fivefold ministry, and are even now being equipped and empowered for the work of service. When I was first called, fulfilling that call seemed absolutely impossible. I simply didn't have what it took. I didn't have the right background, the right education, the right training or the right experience. I could see others fulfilling such a call, but not myself. I had none of the serious requirements. Paul went on to address such concerns:

For ye see your calling, brethren, how that not many wise men after the flesh, not many mighty, not many noble, are called: but God hath chosen the foolish things of the world to confound the wise; and God hath chosen the weak things of the world to confound the things which are mighty; and the base things of the world, and things which are despised, hath God

> *chosen, yea, and things which are not, to bring*
> *to nought things that are.* 1 Corinthians 1:26

Any and every power of this world will be overcome by the power of Christ. Why? Verse 29 reveals the why of it:

> *That no flesh should glory in his presence.*
> 1 Corinthians 1:29

God uses the simplicity and the foolishness of who we are, He uses the weak, and He even uses broken vessels. In the midst of our weakness, He shows Himself strong. His power is the very anointing of God that breaks the yoke.

As noted, Paul was very well educated, even religiously so. He had sat at the feet of one of the greatest Jewish teachers of his time. But when he launched out to begin His ministry, he didn't preach in his own understanding. He preached the presence and the power of God. That seemed like silliness to some, but he insisted on leaning on that truth instead of his own understanding. And you and I need to do the same.

This does not mean that we can do without solid training and good teaching or that we don't need to develop a spiritual understanding. It does not mean that we can ignore opportunities to serve as interns, spending time working out the important elements of our faith. These are all important parts of our preparation.

From the moment your gifting is recognized by God and man, then begins the discipling process. You need to align yourself with qualified teachers who can help you to hone your gifts and calling. They can equip you and help to shape you into strong believers, and they can give you a platform that you can work from to begin your spiritual development.

Giving someone else a platform seems difficult for many. It is never easy for them to sit back while you occupy "their" platform. Some of this is natural. We all want to work for God, but we can't all do it at the same time. Someone has to give way in order for others to emerge.

If you are reluctant to give others an opportunity, recognize some degree of ego and flesh at work and take authority over it. Begin to think Kingdom thoughts and do Kingdom acts. What is best for the Kingdom is for all to have a part, for all to grow and develop. If you always hog the limelight, you are hindering the development of the next generation, and that may be your legacy.

Tell your flesh to submit to the will of God, and then be happy with that decision. What is best for the Kingdom is best for all of God's Kingdom people. Is it best for you? Of course. The Scriptures are clear:

> *It is more blessed to give than to receive.*
>
> Acts 20:35

More blessed. So, yes, this is best for you too.

This Kingdom thinking is opposite to the thinking of the world. Out there, it is all about what you can gather, what you can get your hands on. With us, the power is in the release, in giving away what has been given to us so that someone else can reach their God-given potential, answer their call and walk in their destiny.

I believe that the Church is slowly turning, but it's a huge vessel, and the turning is very slow. Some are coming to understand that the purpose of the fivefold ministry is not to be recognized or elevated, but rather to equip the humblest saints, so that they, too, can do the work of ministry.

There is power in the cross and in the simplicity of who you are, your calling and your anointing. The anointing is not complicated; its simple. When I minister prophetically under the anointing, that's simple. It's easy. If you would come to me and begin to tell me all of your spiritual needs, asking me to lift them up in prayer, by the time you had listed four or five of them, I would no longer be able to remember the first thing you wanted ne to pray for. When I am in the Spirit and pray what the Spirit leads me, things get done more efficiently. When you don't know what to say, say whatever God is saying. He hasn't stopped talking, and He hasn't stopped healing. Prophesy what He says, exhort and encourage with all long suffering and doctrine, and in this way we will be encouraging one another prophetically.

I love the power of Philippians 2. There is some language here that we use often in our everyday Christian experience because it is so powerful. Paul wrote:

> *Let this mind be in you, which was also in Christ Jesus: who, being in the form of God, thought it not robbery to be equal with God: but made himself of no reputation, and took upon him the form of a servant, and made in the likeness of men: and being found in fashion as a man, he humbled himself, and became obedient unto death, even the death of the cross.*
>
> Philippians 2:5-8

Even the death of the cross. In this chapter, we're dealing with the power of the cross, so we have to remember that one of the things that happened at the cross was death. I cannot tell you everything that God wants to do in and through you in the coming weeks, months and years, but I can tell you that before it all happens, there must be a death. Jesus had to die to give us life, and our flesh has to die if we are to carry His life to others. The cross speaks of death.

The power of the cross can kill sin and self. Paul wrote:

> *I die daily.*　　　　　　1 Corinthians 15:31

That may not be a very popular message, but it's a necessary one. It declares what Jesus said we must do:

> *And he that taketh not his cross, and followeth after me, is not worthy of me.*
> Matthew 10:38

> *Then said Jesus unto his disciples, If any man will come after me, let him deny himself, and take up his cross, and follow me.*
> Matthew 16:24

This is something that must be done on a regular basis, preferably daily. The power of the cross is not just for the moment I am saved; it has keeping power for the days, weeks, months and years that follow.

The power of the cross is even more important for those who are called to ministry. Ministering in the gifts and power of the Spirit, which are grace gifts, requires access to the work of the cross. How do we get more grace?

> *God resisteth the proud, and giveth grace to the humble.* 1 Peter 5:5

When there is pride in us, our holy God is repelled. When there is humility in us, it draws His presence. Humility allows for the release of grace in our lives and the working of the power of the cross. Therefore, humility is an important key when looking for the power that comes though the cross.

What happened on the cross? Christ overcame, and His death provides us the power to overcome. What He did there was not for Himself. It was for you and me. His obedience in answering the call to death on the cross paved the way for us to be victorious every single day.

What Jesus suffered was unspeakable. He suffered pain, humiliation and betrayal and had to do it all alone. He therefore understands all that we go through and has made a way for us to overcome, just as He overcame:

> *Wherefore God also hath highly exalted him, and given him a name which is above every other name: that at the name of Jesus every knee should bow, of things in heaven, and things in the earth, and things under the earth; and that every tongue should confess that Jesus Christ is Lord, to the glory of God the Father.*
>
> Philippians 2:9-10

He is our Lord. Don't confuse this with Jesus being our Savior. Our salvation comes when we believe in our heart and confess with our mouth that God raised Jesus Christ from the dead. In other words, when we believe in what happened at the cross and in the resurrection and act on it. It is though faith in the work of the cross that we can be reconciled to God. So, confess Him as Savior, but also confess Him as Lord.

What does this mean? It means that we are listening to Him by the power of the Holy Spirit, and we will be obedient to what He wants us to be and to do. That walk of obedience may be difficult, but it's the greatest walk any of us could ever make. That was the walk Jesus made from the manger to the grave.

Jesus began the last stages of that walk in the Garden of Gethsemane. He knew His destiny and understood the Scriptures. He knew Isaiah 53:

> *Who hath believed our report? and to whom is the arm of the LORD revealed? For he shall grow up before him as a tender plant, and as a root out of a dry ground: he hath no form nor comeliness; and when we shall see him, there is no beauty that we should desire him. He is despised and rejected of men; a man of sorrows, and acquainted with grief: and we hid as it were our faces from him; he was despised, and we esteemed him not.*
>
> *Surely he hath borne our griefs, and carried our sorrows: yet we did esteem him stricken, smitten of God, and afflicted. But he was wounded for our transgressions, he was bruised for our iniquities: the chastisement of our peace was upon him; and with his stripes we are healed. All we like sheep have gone astray; we have turned every one to his own way; and the LORD hath laid on him the iniquity of us all.*
>
> *He was oppressed, and he was afflicted, yet he*

opened not his mouth: he is brought as a lamb to the slaughter, and as a sheep before her shearers is dumb, so he openeth not his mouth. He was taken from prison and from judgment: and who shall declare his generation? for he was cut off out of the land of the living: for the transgression of my people was he stricken. And he made his grave with the wicked, and with the rich in his death; because he had done no violence, neither was any deceit in his mouth.

Yet it pleased the LORD to bruise him; he hath put him to grief: when thou shalt make his soul an offering for sin, he shall see his seed, he shall prolong his days, and the pleasure of the LORD shall prosper in his hand. He shall see of the travail of his soul, and shall be satisfied: by his knowledge shall my righteous servant justify many; for he shall bear their iniquities. Therefore will I divide him a portion with the great, and he shall divide the spoil with the strong; because he hath poured out his soul unto death: and he was numbered with the transgressors; and he bare the sin of many, and made intercession for the transgressors.

Isaiah 53:1-12

Jesus knew that evil men would pluck out His beard, spit on Him, beat Him, place a crown of thorns on His head, that He would be shamed and embarrassed, and that He would die the horrible and feared death of the cross hung between two thieves. It was the most degrading thing that could be done to a man. It is very possible that He was hanging there naked and vulnerable, and what is sure is that He was being crucified by the very people He had been called to save.

Jesus knew all of this when He was there praying in the Garden, and He began His death right there. Despite knowing it all and what it meant, He prayed:

Not my will, but thine, be done.   Luke 22:42

In that moment, death began to take hold of our Lord, and you and I have not died to self until it is no longer our own will that is motivating our words and deeds. If we are still making the decisions about where we want to go and what we want to do, our flesh is still ruling us. What happened to obedience? The Old Testament prophet Samuel declared that obedience is *"better than sacrifice"*:

And Samuel said, Hath the LORD as great delight in burnt offerings and sacrifices, as in

> *obeying the voice of the LORD? Behold, to obey*
> *is better than sacrifice, and to hearken than the*
> *fat of rams.* 1 Samuel 15:22

Yes, obedience is better than sacrifice, and it was obedience that took Jesus to the cross. Today, in our modern world, with all of its benefits and comforts, we often try to stay as far away from the cross as possible. We don't feel comfortable when we are no longer in charge. But, let me tell you: if you are still in charge of your life, you're in trouble! If you are still making your own decisions, you're headed in the wrong direction!

We have to know ourselves, that we are somehow rooted in evil, and we must insist on being led by the Spirit of God and walking in obedience to Him every single hour of every single day. This takes the work of the cross in us.

You and I are still human beings, and we must resist the tendency to insist on being in control. As Americans, we love to be in control, so submission to the will of God is our only answer. Death to self is our only solution. There is no other way to Heaven.

Get ready for this endurance walk because we all have to go the way of the cross. We must go there again and again, and there is no other recourse but obedience.

Jesus linked obedience to love:

If ye love me, keep my commandments.
John 14:15

Loving God is not a two-step dance. It involves making the hard decisions and, when necessary, the hard sacrifices. Love means making Him Lord of all. I'm afraid that there are many people sitting in churches on Sunday who have not yet made Christ Lord of all. Why do I say that? Just look at their lives. It's easy to see that they are still lord over their own futures. Full submission to Christ is love's requirement.

We must come to understand how the power of the cross is to be made manifest in us. Jesus said:

And he that taketh not his cross, and followeth after me, is not worthy of me. Matthew 10:38

This is self-denial. This is taking up your cross to follow Him. This is answering the call with all of your determination, all of your resources, all of your time and talents and all of your strength. When people wait until the very last possible minute to pick up their cross, that is not only dangerous; it is sad.

As a pastor, I have been with people who were dying. I had tried to minister to them weeks or months before, and they were not yet ready to surrender all to Christ. Now, they had finally done it. Thank God that they had the chance to surrender, but I have to ask myself why they waited so long? They lost out on the best life had to offer by delaying their visit to the cross until the very last moment.

Christ must be your highest priority, and when He is, you can access the power of God. It takes a humbling to get there, but the rewards are immeasurable. God knows so much more than we know, so why are we still making our own choices? Obeying Him is the best choice. That brings us to an understanding of the power of the cross.

Jesus suffered on His way to the cross. Then He suffered the humiliations of Isaiah 53, and you and I also have some things to bear on our way to total victory in Christ. The cross is prophetic, the cross is symbolic, and the cross is real. The cross has become such a powerful symbol that the enemy, the spirit of Antichrist, the spirit of chaos and anarchy that has been released across the earth and especially here in America today, hates it and attacks it at every turn.

The Power of His Cross

If the world hates the cross, that should tell us something. This is a powerful symbol of the power of God made real in our daily lives. There is a concerted effort to remove the cross from all public places, from every seat of government. The enemy calls it foolishness, and the Antichrist insists that it be removed from all venues of education, healthcare and anything else important to the believer. That cross, wherever you see it anywhere in the world, is a symbol of the power and the presence and the reality of Jesus Christ. It is a symbol of His Lordship over all of humanity. Therefor, when you fall in love with that cross, you, too, will be attacked. When you love the cross, you will quickly learn who is your friend and who is your enemy. And it doesn't take long to realize that there are more enemies than friends.

It would be surprising if we somehow had a legitimate vote here in the U.S. and Canada concerning the cross. The truth is that our countries have become major mission fields. Personally, I'm for some restraint at our borders, but I am also in favor of more immigration. We just need God to bring in the right people. Many Hindu and Moslem immigrants have been able to hear the Gospel and turn to Christ. In their own countries, preaching the Christian Gospel was limited or forbidden altogether. They had to come here to find salvation through Jesus. Here they experienced the power of the cross of Christ. Thank God for that.

The cross is a symbol of victory. Jesus suffered the worst defeat any man could suffer, but He turned it all around. He went to the cross like a sheep before the shearer:

> *As a sheep before her shearers is dumb, so he openeth not his mouth.*   Isaiah 53:7

He knew what men intended to do to Him, but He kept silent, not uttering a word of protest. He refused to defend Himself, and He did it all for you and me. Yes, there is power in the cross! That power begins with our obedience and our sacrifice.

There is nothing wrong with pursuing a nice career. God has that for you. But don't ever let that career come between you and God. Serve Him above all else. Put nothing before Him. Putting anything before God is idolatry. It might be a love for riches, it might be a love for a person, or it might be a love for something else. Love Jesus above all else always.

Never require that anyone love you more than they love God. Never require that anyone obey you more than they obey God. And never require that anyone serve you more than they serve God. After all, you can't save them, so why bind them to you in this way? We can have a happy home and work life and still do the will of God and let others do the same.

Parents, don't let you children make you their god. You can't even save yourself, much less save your children. Turn them on to God. Let them know that happiness and success reside only in knowing Him, in experiencing the place of the cross, the place of surrender, the place of sacrifice, the place of obedience. This is the place where you lay down your worldly wisdom and embrace godly thoughts. Jesus is ready to meet you at the cross.

We are all ministers, and we need to understand the priesthood of the believer. From the moment we said Yes to Jesus Christ, a ministry was birthed in us, and now we are kings and priests unto God through Jesus. We are a royal priesthood and a holy nation and every single one of us has a ministry. Every one of us has a call.

From the moment that Jesus came into our lives, we were born again and possessed a new DNA, a spiritual DNA. Therefore, we need to begin to manifest who we are in Christ. We need to know who we are and know what we are called to do. We need to know where the power of God is and how to begin to access it.

We access the power of God the very same way we access His salvation—by faith, by declaration and by proclamation. As I noted in my introduction, God has said that if we declare a thing, He will establish it for us. In other words, there is power in your tongue. You can make bold declarations, and when you do, God will establish them for you.

It's time to begin to access God's power, and it is done by first believing in your heart. Faith is an expression of what is inside of you. Faith may be a declaration that you make, but first you have to believe it in your heart and know that the power of the resurrection is your portion.

Christ is alive, and the Hope of Glory lives inside of us. Furthermore, He will never leave us or forsake us. He goes with us wherever we go, and in our weakness, He will show Himself strong. Oh, we need the power of God. We need the strength of the Gospel. We need the power of the cross, and we can access it by faith. What are you waiting for? Start contending today for *His Light, His Power, His Presence, His Glory.*

Father,

I declare Your Word now concerning the power that is in the cross. I release it right now over each of us. Help us to move into a place of strong obedience to You. May we obey You in the little things and also in the larger things.

I bind the spirit of fear, worry and doubt. I bind the spirits of fear of poverty, fear of man, fear of loss and fear of failure. I bind you now, in Jesus' name, and I declare victory through the power of the cross of Jesus Christ. Lord, let that power now begin to come alive in our hearts, that we may know You and the power of Your resurrection.

Oh, Living God, the only true God, may we come to know You more! Even in the midst of our mutual sufferings, may we know You! Help us to know You more fully. And we'll give You the glory, the honor and the praise.

Right now, Father, I release over those who are reading these pages a fresh anointing, a fresh new word, and a fresh blessing.

In Jesus' name,
Amen!

THE POWER OF THE CROSS IS NOT JUST FOR THE MOMENT I AM SAVED; IT HAS KEEPING POWER FOR THE DAYS, WEEKS, MONTHS AND YEARS THAT FOLLOW!

Chapter 3

The Power of His Resurrection

Jesus said unto her, I am the resurrection, and the life: he that believeth in me, though he were dead, yet shall he live: and whosoever liveth and believeth in me shall never die. Believest thou this? She saith unto him, Yea, Lord: I believe that thou art the Christ, the Son of God, which should come into the world.

John 11:25-27

Yes, there is power in His resurrection. We need to know that there is power in His resurrection, and then we need to appropriate that power. Not only is the resurrection powerful. Jesus said that He *was* the resurrection and the life. Today we, the Body of Christ, need to experience resurrection power in order to fulfill our prophetic mandate.

Believing that God raised Jesus from the dead is another of the foundation stones of our faith:

> *That if thou shalt confess with thy mouth the Lord Jesus, and shalt believe in thine heart that God hath raised him from the dead, thou shalt be saved. For with the heart man believeth unto righteousness; and with the mouth confession is made unto salvation.*
> Romans 10:9-10

The resurrection is the power of God to save, the power of God to give life to dead things. If there had been no resurrection, there could not have been no salvation. Paul said it this way:

> *But if there be no resurrection of the dead, then is Christ not risen: and if Christ be not risen, then is our preaching vain, and your faith is also vain.*   1 Corinthians 15:13-14

Even our faith, Paul said, is vain (producing no results, useless), if there is no resurrection.

The resurrection is the power to heal. Notice what the disciples of Jesus said:

The Power of His Resurrection

Be it known unto you all, and to all the people of Israel, that by the name of Jesus Christ of Nazareth, whom ye crucified, whom God raised from the dead, even by him doth this man stand here before you whole. This is the stone which was set at nought of you builders, which is become the head of the corner. Neither is there salvation in any other: for there is none other name under heaven given among men, whereby we must be saved. Acts 4:10-12

The fact that Jesus had been raised from the dead gave Him unparalleled legitimacy. The resurrection was what declared Jesus to be the Son of God:

Concerning his Son Jesus Christ our Lord, which was made of the seed of David according to the flesh; and declared to be the Son of God with power, according to the spirit of holiness, by the resurrection from the dead.

Romans 1:3-4

And with great power gave the apostles witness of the resurrection of the Lord Jesus: and great grace was upon them all. Acts 4:33

As noted in an earlier chapter, Paul's heartcry in Philippians 3:10 was, *"that I may know him in the power of his resurrection"*:

> *That I may know him, and the power of his resurrection, and the fellowship of his sufferings, being made conformable unto his death; if by any means I might attain unto the resurrection of the dead. Not as though I had already attained, either were already perfect: but I follow after, if that I may apprehend that for which also I am apprehended of Christ Jesus.*
>
> Philippians 3:10-12

The Word of God tells us that Christ was the firstfruits of the resurrection. This means that you and I will also have a resurrection.

The resurrection speaks to us of the timing of events, even of the end of time. The Father raised Christ from the dead on the third day, and Peter made this analogy:

> *But, beloved, be not ignorant of this one thing, that one day is with the Lord as a thousand years, and a thousand years as one day.*
>
> 2 Peter 3:8

The Power of His Resurrection

It was early on the morning of the third day, when the Father raised Jesus from the dead in resurrection power. This, beloved, is the third day of time (the third millennium), and that means it is early in the morning of the third day and God will prophetically raise up the Body of Christ. It's time for you and me to arise and shine. Can you hear God's resurrection call?

> *Arise, shine; for thy light is come, and the glory of the LORD is risen upon thee.*   Isaiah 60:1

There's power in the resurrection, and we need resurrection power. Therefore, we need to know how to access that power.

Just as the Father sent resurrection life into the dead body of Jesus and He came forth from the grave, now it will happen symbolically, as God raises up the Body of Christ, His Church. What will result? We will receive body ministry and a movement in the Spirit throughout the Body. Resurrection power will come to restore life to a damaged and broken Church. Thank God for His resurrection power. It is one more part of *His Light, His Power, His Presence, His Glory.*

I speak now to the remnant, to the Bride that comes out of the Body, to the prophetic end-time army of God. "Body of Christ, come forth! Awaken, arise and shine! This is your moment. I declare resurrection power over you right now, that life would come to the driest parts of your limbs and that you would blossom and bear fruit."

I prophetically speak to the dry bones: "Hear the Word of the Lord. Behold, in this hour, the very breath of God will enter into you, and you shall live."

I prophesy unto the wind and say, "Breathe upon these bones and bring forth resurrection power, now. In the name that is above every other name, the name of Jesus Christ of Nazareth, I declare life to return to dead dreams and visions, and I declare new hope and life more abundant!"

In Jesus' name,
Amen!

JUST AS THE FATHER SENT RESURRECTION LIFE INTO THE DEAD BODY OF JESUS AND HE CAME FORTH FROM THE GRAVE, NOW IT WILL HAPPEN SYMBOLICALLY, AS GOD RAISES UP THE BODY OF CHRIST, HIS CHURCH!

Chapter 4

The Power of His Blood

This is my blood of the covenant, which is poured out for many for the forgiveness of sins.
Matthew 26:28, NIV

There is power in the blood of Jesus. We first have to know that there is power in His blood, and then we have to appropriate that power.

Not everybody is saved, and the very thought that everybody is saved is nonsense. It is only those who call on the name of the Lord, only those who believe in the power of the resurrection, only those who have had His precious blood applied to their hearts who will be saved.

Have you been washed by the precious blood of Jesus? He died on the cross for all of us, shedding His blood for our sins. But we are not just automatically saved. We are saved when we apply our faith to what He has done. We must appropriate the power of the blood, just as we do every other provision of our faith. We declare with our mouth the Lordship of Jesus Christ and believe in our heart that God raised Him from the dead, and we are saved. Use that same faith to appropriate the power of the blood in your life.

The blood has power to purge us from dead works so we can serve the living God:

> *For if the blood of bulls and of goats, and the ashes of an heifer sprinkling the unclean, sanctifieth to the purifying of the flesh: how much more shall the blood of Christ, who through the eternal Spirit offered himself without spot to God, purge your conscience from dead works to serve the living God?*
>
> Hebrews 9:13-14

Our understanding of the power of the blood gives us the ability to shed ourselves of fleshly works, rituals, sacrifices and sacraments, so that we may serve Him and worship Him in Spirit and in truth. What is needed is not our own righteousness but, rather, the righteousness of Christ in us.

According to Paul's teachings in Ephesians, our very redemption is though Christ's blood, as is also the forgiveness of sin. He said:

> *In whom we have redemption through his blood,*
> *the forgiveness of sins, according to the riches*
> *of his grace; wherein he hath abounded toward*
> *us in all wisdom and prudence.*
>
> Ephesians 1:7-8

It is the power of the blood that allows us to walk in the light, having fellowship with one another and being purged from all sin.

John taught:

> *But if we walk in the light, as he is in the light,*
> *we have fellowship with one another, and the*
> *blood of Jesus, his Son, purifies us from all sin.*
>
> 1 John 1:7

It is the power of the blood that unites us in true fellowship, as brothers and sisters, and that fellowship can only be shared by those who are washed in the blood of the Lamb.

It is the blood that gives us power to overcome. John the Revelator recorded:

The Power of His Blood

And I heard a loud voice saying in heaven, Now is come salvation, and strength, and the kingdom of our God, and the power of his Christ: for the accuser of our brethren is cast down, which accused them before our God day and night. And they overcame him by the blood of the Lamb, and by the word of their testimony; and they loved not their lives unto the death.

Revelation 12:10-11

This is the way we overcome the enemy and his attacks. The blood of Jesus applied to our hearts releases the needed strength.

Another important passage related to the blood of Jesus (and already alluded to) is found in Romans:

That if thou shalt confess with thy mouth the Lord Jesus, and shalt believe in thine heart that God hath raised him from the dead, thou shalt be saved. For with the heart man believeth unto righteousness; and with the mouth confession is made unto salvation. Romans 10:9-10

These two scriptures give us much insight into how to appropriate and apply the power of the blood of Jesus to our lives, not just for our initial salvation experience, but also for every area of our daily lives. We believe with our hearts and then declare it with our lips. We can plead the power of the blood over every situation and every need of our lives.

Let me give you some examples of how I use this power in my everyday life:

First, I use the power of the blood in my thought life. Thoughts are powerful. God's Word shows us:

> *As he [a man] thinketh in his heart, so is he.*
> Proverbs 23:7

He is what he thinks. Wow!

Jesus said that if a man looks on a woman and desires to have her, he is already guilty of adultery with her in his heart:

> *Whosoever looketh on a woman to lust after her*
> *hath committed adultery with her already in his*
> *heart.* Matthew 5:28

Sin as a deed is not the only kind of sin. We sometimes sin with our thoughts, and we sometimes sin with our words. Let me clarify that.

When a wrong thought pops into my head, I don't necessarily consider that to be a sin. That thought may have been put there by the enemy to temp me, or it could be the result of things going on around me or something I heard someone say or something I saw. But once I realize it's there, I need to deal with that thought quickly and effectively. So what can I do? I plead the blood of Jesus over my mind, believing that it has the power to cleanse my thoughts, and I declare with my mouth that it is so. I repent for that thought, and ask God to cleanse me from it. Here again is the promise of 1 John 1:

> *But if we walk in the light, as he is in the light, we have fellowship one with another, and the blood of Jesus Christ his Son cleanseth us from all sin. If we say that we have no sin, we deceive ourselves, and the truth is not in us. If we confess our sins, he is faithful and just to forgive us our sins, and to cleanse us from all unrighteousness.* 1 John 1:7-9

What a powerful promise! If I confess my sin, God is faithful and just to forgive me. But He doesn't just forgive me of that sin; He also cleanses me of all unrighteousness. Oh, thank God, the blood purges me, cleanses me of any and all unrighteousness.

If an unhealthy thought seems to persist, I may also use the power to bind and loose found in Matthew 16. This is another of our weapons of warfare and keys to the Kingdom:

> *And I will give unto thee the keys of the kingdom of heaven: and whatsoever thou shalt bind on earth shall be bound in heaven: and whatsoever thou shalt loose on earth shall be loosed in heaven.* Matthew 16:19

By faith, I believe in my heart, and by faith I declare with my mouth, and the power of the blood of Jesus is applied to any and every situation. I plead the blood of Jesus over my problems, over any hindrances, over my thoughts, my feelings and emotions, over family issues and over any attack or assignment of the enemy.

I plead the blood of Jesus over the door jams of my home or anyplace else I happen to be staying at the moment, by believing and then declaring the power of Jesus' blood in that place. As we have seen, when I declare a thing, my heavenly Father will establish it for me. Therefore, when I believe it and declare it, it is done!

God has declared that life is in the blood:

The Power of His Blood

For the life of the flesh is in the blood: and I have given it to you upon the altar to make an atonement for your souls: for it is the blood that maketh an atonement for the soul. Leviticus 17:11

Sometimes, if I feel that something has died—a hope, a dream, a promise or a feeling, for instance—and I want to bring it back, I plead the blood of Jesus over it, knowing that there is life in the blood. I understand and believe in the power that's in the blood. Do you? Then what are you waiting for? Begin to contend today for *His Light, His Power, His Presence, His Glory.*

In the name of Jesus Christ and by the power of the Holy Spirit, I plead the precious blood of Jesus Christ over you right now: over your mind, over your body, over your emotions, over every part of your being. Over your family, over everything and everyone that's near and dear to you. Over every problematic situation, over every

difficult circumstance, over every need and over every relationship.

I plead the blood of Jesus over your finances, your health and your career. I bind every attack and assignment of the enemy, and I declare life, freedom, hope, joy and prosperity over you and your family.

Amen!

THIS IS THE WAY WE OVERCOME THE ENEMY AND HIS ATTACKS. THE BLOOD OF JESUS APPLIED TO OUR HEARTS RELEASES THE NEEDED STRENGTH!

Chapter 5

The Power of His Name

Wherefore God also hath highly exalted him, and given him a name which is above every name: that at the name of Jesus every knee should bow, of things in heaven, and things in earth, and things under the earth; and that every tongue should confess that Jesus Christ is Lord, to the glory of God the Father.

Philippians 2:9-11

There is power in His name. If fact, there is power in any name. Names have meaning, and every time a name is called, that particular meaning is evoked. If a daughter is named Ailsa, for example, every time Ailsa is called, the person calling her is saying, "Consecrated One." That's powerful, isn't it!

The Power of His Name

But there is another name that is even more powerful. It is the name above every other name, the name of Jesus. One day every knee will bow to that name and every tongue will confess that He is indeed Lord.

In Hebrew, His name was Yeshua, from the definitive verb that meant "to rescue, to deliver." Among the Jewish people of the Second-Temple Period, that name Yeshua was a very common one. It was actually a shortened form of the name Joshua. But there was only one Jesus of Nazareth, Son of God. He is the Great Deliverer, and there is power in His name.

Even today, in the Catholic countries, many parents name one of their sons Jesus. But none of these Jesuses is *the* Jesus, the One who bears that matchless name and its power. In that name is the power to heal, to save and to deliver. Paul wrote to the early Roman believers:

> *For whosoever shall call upon the name of the Lord shall be saved. How then shall they call on him in whom they have not believed? and how shall they believe in him on whom they have not heard? and how shall they hear without a preacher?* Romans 10:13-14

One of the ways to declare the power of the name of the Lord is to preach and to teach in His name. Paul went on:

> *And how shall they preach, except they be sent? as it is written, How beautiful are the feet of them that preach the gospel of peace, and bring glad tidings of good things!*   Romans 10:15

For a moment, let's look back at verse 9 again:

> *That if thou shalt confess with thy mouth the Lord Jesus, and shalt believe in thine heart that God hath raised him from the dead, thou shalt be saved.*   Romans 10:9

Salvation is in the declaration of that name. Salvation is in the name of the Lord. But it's more than salvation. There is also deliverance in the name of the Lord.

Mark 16 gives us a mandate to go to the nations. There it says:

> *And he said unto them, Go ye into all the world, and preach the gospel to every creature. He that believeth and is baptized shall be saved; but he*

that believeth not shall be damned. And these signs shall follow them that believe; In my name shall they cast out devils; they shall speak with new tongues; they shall take up serpents; and if they drink of any deadly thing, it shall not harm them; they shall lay hands on the sick, and they shall recover. Mark 16:15-18

Yes, there is salvation in the name of Jesus, but there is also healing and deliverance in that name. He said, *"In my name shall they cast out devils."* There is freedom in His name. His name gives us power to set captives free, and His name empowers the captives to be set free and to remain free.

There is even power in our simple act of gathering in His name. Jesus said:

For where two or three are gathered together in my name, there am I in the midst of them.
Matthew 18:20

The power is not in the act of gathering itself. It is in the act of gathering in His name. There is power in that name, power to save, power to heal and power to deliver.

His name is to be used in prayer:

His Light, His Power, His Presence and His Glory

And whatsoever ye shall ask in my name, that will I do, that the Father may be glorified in the Son. If ye shall ask any thing in my name, I will do it. John 14:13-14

The name of Jesus empowers your prayers. It brings His presence, it brings His glory, and that is what changes us. We simply must have an understanding of the power that is in the name of Jesus if we are to be God's ambassadors here on Earth.

All power and authority have been given to us, but we need to know how to access that power. We have to know, first and foremost, that it belongs to us, that it has been given to us. Then we need to know how to access it.

The way you access the power in the name of Jesus is by declaration and proclamation. I declare that His power is on my tongue. I declare that His presence is with me, by faith, for He said it would be so. Again, the Lord has promised that if I declare and decree a thing, He will establish it for me. So, when I act in faith and declare a thing in the name of Jesus, I don't have to pray, "God, are You here? Are You hearing me? I can't feel You."

If I prayed like that, I think He would answer, "Haven't you read what I said? Do you not know My

Word? I have said that I am not a man that I could lie. I said that when you gather in My name, I will be with you. So, yes, I am here. Why do you doubt it?"

God is who He said He is, and He means what He says He means. Who is He? First, He is the Great I Am. When Moses asked God, *"Who should I tell the people sent me?"* (see Exodus 3:13), God answered:

> *I Am That I Am ... , Thus shalt thou say unto the children of Israel, I Am hath sent me unto you.* Exodus 3:14

Who is I AM? He is a great big God who fills the entire Universe, even though His name is so small. I AM ... how simple, but that is a very powerful name! It means "I am anything you will ever need. Where I AM is nothing is absent. Whatever you need is supplied. When I AM is in your midst, you are whole. You see, it's not the size of the name that counts, but the power of that name.

Again, this is power to save and power to heal. When the disciples performed a healing miracle on a lame man who had been in this condition for many years, they were called to account by the people. Peter explained it this way.

Ye men of Israel, why marvel ye at this? or why look ye so earnestly on us, as though by our own power or holiness we had made this man to walk? The God of Abraham, and of Isaac, and of Jacob, the God of our fathers, hath glorified his Son Jesus; whom ye delivered up, and denied him in the presence of Pilate, when he was determined to let him go. But ye denied the Holy One and the Just, and desired a murderer to be granted unto you; and killed the Prince of life, whom God hath raised from the dead; whereof we are witnesses. And his name through faith in his name hath made this man strong, whom ye see and know: yea, the faith which is by him hath given him this perfect soundness in the presence of you all. Acts 3:12-16

The disciples could not take the glory for this amazing miracle of healing. It was done by the power of and in the name of Jesus. He is the Healer; we're not the Healer. It is God and God alone who heals; we are just vessels that He chooses to use to accomplish His healing. He is the very essence of healing.

Next, something terrible happened. The religious leaders of the day came and took the disciples to prison, accusing them of many things. They were held that night, and then the next day, the following occurred:

And when they had set them in the midst, they asked, By what power, or by what name, have ye done this? Then Peter, filled with the Holy Ghost, said unto them, Ye rulers of the people, and elders of Israel, if we this day be examined of the good deed done to the impotent man, by what means he is made whole; be it known unto you all, and to all the people of Israel, that by the name of Jesus Christ of Nazareth, whom ye crucified, whom God raised from the dead, even by him doth this man stand here before you whole. This is the stone which was set at nought of you builders, which is become the head of the corner. Neither is there salvation in any other: for there is none other name under heaven given among men, whereby we must be saved. Acts 4:7-12

Verse 18 records:

And they called them, and commanded them not to speak at all nor teach in the name of Jesus.
Acts 4:18

Why? Because it was obvious that this name was very powerful. The religious leaders didn't just tell them to stop preaching. They had to stop preaching *in that name*. And did the disciples stop preaching in or otherwise using the name of Jesus? Of course not. They continued to speak in His name. His name is too powerful to ignore.

Today, especially in the Western Hemisphere, there is a tendency to restrict the use of the name, Jesus. Most people don't mind if you mention God. After all, you could be referring to any god. But if you use the name of Jesus, people are offended. It's like raising a war cry.

Our God is a man of war and when you declare the name of Jesus Christ, you are saying it's time for war. You are calling on the name of the Great Warrior, the great Man of War. His name is the Lord, and there is power in that name.

As noted in an earlier chapter, there is a push to do away with the symbol of the cross in all public places. In the same way, there is a concerted effort underway to restrict the mention of the name of Jesus,that name above every other name. Why? Because there is such great power in that name.

God had other names in ancient times. Among the first names used for Him were *El* ("God"), *Eloah*

("God"), *Elohim* ("Gods," showing His multifaceted nature). Another of the first names the Hebrews knew God by was *El Shaddai,* meaning the God of more than enough.

Another of the ancient names of God was *Yahweh*, or Jehovah, as it was transliterated. This name was most often translated simply as *Lord* in the English versions of the Bible.

This name also has many variations. There was, for instance, *Jehovah-Jireh*, God My Provider or God Who Supplies:

> *And Abraham said, My son, God will provide himself a lamb for a burnt offering.*
>
> Genesis 22:8

You and I must know that God Himself is our Source; otherwise we might come to think that some man is our source. If we "kiss up to" a boss, thinking that he or she is our source and our career and paycheck depend on maintaining a good relationship with them, we may become dependent upon that person and not on God Himself.

God is not calling us to be independent; He wants us to be interconnected or interdependent within the Body of Christ. But we can never replace Him as our

Source of all things, and to do so is idolatry. Is He Jehovah-Jireh in your life?

Jesus spent a lot of time with His disciples and had some very deep conversations with them. On one of those occasions, He asked them:

> *Whom do men say that I am?*   Mark 8:27

They answered:

> *John the Baptist; but some say, Elias; and others, One of the prophets.*   Mark 8:28

Jesus was leading up to a more important question, and He asked it now:

> *But whom say ye that I am?*   Mark 8:29

Peter spoke up and said,

> *Thou art the Christ.*   Mark 8:29

Who is He to you? Who is your teacher Who is your savior? Who is your lord? Who is your provider? To some, He is definitely their savior, and they recognize Him as such, but it soon becomes apparent that

He is not their lord. Some don't believe that divine healing is for today, so He is not their healer. Some lean much too heavily on other men, so they don't really know God in His fullness. Are you satisfied to forever be dependant upon others? Or will you declare to all that He is your Jehovah-Jireh, your Provider? He promised:

> *But my God shall supply all your need according to his riches in glory by Christ Jesus.*
>
> Philippians 4:19

Who is this God? Jehovah-Jireh is His name.

The marriage relationship is so important, but even in my marriage, I cannot depend solely on my lovely wife. Every morning, when I wake up, I must depend on my God. Mave could have a bad day, but I couldn't allow that to dictate how my day will go. I have to know who I am and whose I am, and that God is my Source.

In the same way, I can have a bad day, so Mave cannot depend solely on me. God is her Source, and that is what dictates how her day will go. If I have a bad day every time Mave has a bad day or she has a bad day every time I do, then we become codependent upon each other, and that is not healthy. Is He your Jehovah-Jireh?

Another of the names for God in ancient times was *Jehovah-Rapha*, God My Healer, or God Who Heals:

> *If thou wilt diligently hearken to the voice of the* Lord *thy God, and wilt do that which is right in his sight, and wilt give ear to his commandments, and keep all his statutes, I will put none of these diseases upon thee, which I have brought upon the Egyptians: for I am the* Lord *that healeth thee.*   Exodus 15:26

"I am the Lord *that healeth thee,"* or Jehovah-Rapha. Do you know Him as your Healer?

As I noted earlier, over the last few years I have had some serious health issues. I have accepted treatment for those issues because I believe in the medical profession. Doctors are dedicated to our health and can be very anointed. God often does His miracles through doctors. However, doctors have their limitations. They can treat me, but they cannot heal me. Only God can do that.

If I cut myself, a doctor can stitch up the wound and give me some antibiotics to keep that wound from becoming infected, but only God can do the actual healing. I'm so glad I know Him as Jehovah Rapha!

Our God is also *Jehovah-Nissi*, the Lord My Banner. We all need to have a banner over us, a banner over our families, a banner over our house, a banner over our land, a banner over our nation. That must become our declaration and proclamation. We will call Him Lord, for He is our Jehovah-Nissi!

I have to know Him in each essence of His name. He is the power behind the name. He is my Jehovah-Jireh, My Provider, because He is the Source of all provision. After all, He owns the cattle on a thousand hills, and all the gold and silver are His. Everything that exists is His, and He is Lord over all. He is Jehovah-Rapha because He alone has the power to heal. He is my Jehovah-Nissi because He is the power behind my banner.

Our God is also *Jehovah-Shalom*, God My Peace. There's such a depth in that word *shalom.* When you go to Israel, you will use this word often. *Shalom*, meaning "peace," has become a common greeting that you use when you meet someone on the street. Each Friday evening, you will greet the sabbath, or *shabbat* in Hebrew, with *Shabbat Shalom.* With these words, you are honoring the Lord and honoring His Sabbath.

Within the scope of that word *shalom* is so much. We need peace in our soul, peace in our bodies, peace in our everyday life. *Shalom* is God's peace, but it also everything that He brings to the plate. The depth of the meaning of this wonderful word is still unfolding, and God is your *Shalom*.

You and I need peace, so we need to know God as our peace. If you don't have peace, let me introduce you to Him, God My Peace.

In the days to come, we will all experience some very difficult times. You'd better get to know the God of peace now, when things are easier. If we can know Him as our peace now in the good times, then, when the bad times come, we will have the assurance of His peace in our hearts.

Our world is headed for total anarchy. Are you ready for that? The chaos will no longer be just in the Middle East or somewhere in Africa. All of our nations are headed for trouble, and we need to be ready for whatever comes. Do you have the peace that passes all understanding?

> *And the peace of God, which passeth all understanding, shall keep your hearts and minds through Christ Jesus.* Philippians 4:7

Our God is also *Jehovah-Ro'i*, God My Shepherd. Do you know my Jehovah-Ro'i? Is He your Shepherd too? He can be.

The Power of His Name

David sang these now famous words:

> *The LORD is my shepherd; I shall not want. He maketh me to lie down in green pastures: he leadeth me beside the still waters. He restoreth my soul: Yea, though I walk through the valley of the shadow of death, I will fear no evil: for thou art with me; thou anointest my head with oil; my cup runneth over. Surely goodness and mercy shall follow me all the days of my life: and I will dwell in the house of the LORD for ever.*
>
> Psalm 23:1-6

We often use this passage when doing a funeral and rightly so, for it is so very beautiful. But this psalm does not speak primarily of death; it's talking about our everyday life. We need the Good Shepherd every single hour of every single day. If you have never known Him in that way, get to know Him today.

Our God is also *Jehovah-Tsidkenu*, God My Righteousness:

> *In his days Judah shall be saved, and Israel shall dwell safely: and this is his name whereby he shall be called, The LORD Our Righteousness.*
>
> Jeremiah 23:6

We have no righteousness apart from Him. He is righteous. He is a good and faithful God. You will always reap what you sow because Jehovah-Tsidkenu is righteous. He cannot be anything but righteous, and He cannot do anything but righteousness. He can never be unfair. He is a just judge because He is totally and forever righteous.

God has been proven righteous time and time again, and He always stands on the side of righteousness. The enemy of the God of Righteousness is sin, and when I stand on the side of sin, I am standing against righteousness, standing against or opposing the God of Righteousness.

Every day, when I begin my activities, I must know that He is righteous and that I will reap what I sow. Otherwise, how could I sow in confidence? I actually believe what the Scriptures teach:

> *Whatsoever a man soweth, that shall he also reap.*   Galatians 6:7

Why do I believe it? Because I understand the righteousness of my God and know that He will do what He says He will do. His words never return void. He said:

So shall my word be that goeth forth out of my mouth: it shall not return unto me void, but it shall accomplish that which I please, and it shall prosper in the thing whereto I sent it.

Isaiah 55:11

He sent His word and healed His people:

He sent his word, and healed them, and delivered them from their destructions.

Psalm 107:20

God's righteous and unfailing words not only bring physical healing; they can also heal our finances. He knows how to do money miracles. When I declare His Word and come into agreement with that Word, I can know that He will not deviate from the righteousness of it.

I can use His righteous words to test the spirits. Therefore that is the first place I go when I have doubts about what spirit is at work in a given situation. The God of Righteousness will not allow me to be deceived. Do you know Him as Jehovah-Tsidkenu?

Our God is also *Jehovah-Shammah*, My God Who Is Present. He is everywhere, and His light shines on us and in us. One of the first decrees I make every day is this: "I love the Lord, and therefore His light shines in me." He is my Jehovah-Shammah.

I have to know God as my light. Otherwise, when I step into any dark place, that darkness may overtake me. When I know that Jehovah-Shammah is within me, I have no fear of going into a dark place. After all, I am taking light with me, my Jehovah-Shammah.

I don't know about you, but I have been in some very dark situations. But, you know what, the light of God shines even brighter in darkness than it does in the light.

I hear people complaining about the place they work—the cursing, the crude jokes, the innuendo. They find it to be a very hard place to work. Why would God send you into a place like that? Could it be because you are filled with light, with God Himself? You were born to shine in darkness. Oh, get to know Jehovah-Shammah, and darkness will no longer affect you.

I've known the Lord now for more than forty years, and He is still revealing Himself more to me every day. I need to know more of His names and understand more of their meanings. His name is powerful.

Why does God have so many different names? Because it is not easy to express the many aspects of

His heart and personality. He is like a multi-faceted gem. For instance, God is both male and female. He said in the book of Genesis that He created man in His image–male and female:

> *So God created man in his own image, in the image of God created he him; male and female created he them.*   Genesis 1:27

Men are created in the image of God, but so are women. We often think of God as Father, but in reality, there is also a mother's heart in Him. He bears both aspects.

I must know Him as the God of Righteousness, but if that is all I know, it may hinder me. If I get constantly beat over the head with calls for repentance, I may not be able to embrace His forgiveness, His and mercy and His grace. He is just as much the God of Grace as He is the God of Righteousness.

Our great God of Grace offers grace to the humble, just as Our God of Righteousness resists the proud. I must learn to access both of these aspects of Jehovah.

When we speak of humility, we don't mean timidity. They are two very different things. God doesn't give us timidity. He gives us a holy boldness to know that we can go in and take the land. Warriors cannot afford to be timid, so God gives us a spirit of boldness, a supernatural boldness. Still, He requires humility from us.

The character of God (and the names that reveal to us that character) will be an ongoing revelation to you as you continue to grow in Him. After forty years, I am not yet done with learning. Tomorrow morning I expect the Lord to show me something new about Himself, about who He is, about what He is doing, and about what He intends to do in that new day. As there is no end to His goodness, this revelation will never stop. He is the inexhaustible God, therefore His names are also without number.

The important thing is to develop a relationship with Him so that we can know Him better. A name is just a name until you actually know the person behind that name. In time, we learn to know God's voice.

Let's say that Pastor Mave (my wife) calls me tomorrow on her cellphone and says, "Hey, honey, how ya doing?" If I would say, "Who's this?" Pastor Mave might come and shake me until my eyeballs fall out. I should know that voice. In fact, because I am hearing that voice every single day, I should know it well. So, when the Lord speaks to me, I don't say, "Who is this?" I know His voice because I have developed a long-term relationship with Him!

The Power of His Name

In the Christian life, everything works from the place of legitimate and intimate relationship with the Living God. Yes, I have to have discernment, but before I even have discernment, I have to have a relationship. God and I have to have a conversation, and that conversation cannot be a one-way street. It must work both ways. I must speak, and I must also listen as He speaks. That's what a relationship is all about, and that is how we learn to hear God's voice and to know Him more intimately.

Sometimes we hear His voice in darkness and sometimes we hear it in light. Sometimes we hear that voice in the midst of chaos. I like to believe that I would be walking across the busy Times Square in New York, I could still hear God's voice and know that it was Him speaking. Sometimes, when I'm in a crowded restaurant or a train station or airport, I hear that voice or God somehow shows me or tells me in my heart to go and see a certain person and share something with them. Sometimes, when I'm in prayer, He will bring someone to my remembrance, and I pray for them. The point is that I have to know the voice of the Lord so that I can respond to Him in obedience. Again, a name is just a name until you actually know the person behind that name.

I love the apostolic prayer of Paul recorded in Ephesians 1:17-18. It is so powerful. What touches me most about this prayer was Paul's desire to know the Lord better. *"That I might know Him,"* as we have seen, was his heartcry. Oh, that we could know our God in the midst of our suffering, that we could know Him in the power of His resurrection.

In truth, that's the only way you can know Jesus. You can't know Him any other way. You can know *about* Him if you just look at a cross or another Christian symbol or read a book about Him, but He has to become your constant companion. His names have to mean something to you personally.

John F. Kennedy was the 35th President of the United States. There are many books written about him and other books written by him, and you can read one of those books and know *about* John F. Kennedy. But unless you had the honor of meeting him before his death in 1963, you cannot know really John F. Kennedy. To you, that is just a name. Actually knowing him required a personal introduction, and that's impossible now because he's gone. You can visit the grave of John F. Kennedy in Arlington Cemetery, but that will not help you to know him. If you didn't have that privilege, it is now impossible.

But I have good news: Jesus' tomb is empty. He is alive, so you can still meet Him and develop an intimate relationship with him. That name Jesus should not just be a name like any other name. That should be your Savior, your personal Friend.

The veil of the Temple has been rent, so no one can put it back together. You and I now have access to the Holy of Holies and to the King of Glory. You can go into God's presence and develop a relationship with the living God. In other words, you can know Jesus and the power of His resurrection and come to know Him in many distinct ways.

Christ suffered for our sins, so He understands anything you might be going through. He suffered to answer His call. He suffered in the Garden of Gethsemane. And He suffered on the cross. He understands all suffering, and He surely understands *your* suffering. He understands persecution. He understands betrayal. There is nothing about you and no aspect of your life that He has not gone through Himself. In fact, the Scriptures assure us that we have suffered nothing that is not *"common to man,"* but that our God will never give us more than we can handle and will always provide us a means of escape:

There hath no temptation taken you but such as is common to man: but God is faithful, who will not suffer you to be tempted above that ye are able; but will with the temptation also make a way to escape, that ye may be able to bear it.

1 Corinthians 10:13

Yes, you need to know more than His name. Know the Person behind that name.

The name of the Lord that I love most is the one John the Revelator used. He said His name was Faithful and True:

And I saw heaven opened, and behold a white horse; and he that sat upon him was called Faithful and True, and in righteousness he doth judge and make war. Revelation 19:11

Faithful and True … That is His name, but it is more than His name. That's who He is for you. He is Faithful and True for you. For me, He is also Faithful and True. He is no respecter of persons:

Then Peter opened his mouth, and said, Of a truth I perceive that God is no respecter of persons. Acts 10:34

Our God is also not a respecter of gender. To both men and women, He is Faithful and True. As He revealed Himself to Steven, He will reveal Himself to you.

Steven was originally chosen as a deacon of the early Church (see Acts 6:5). Very quickly, however, he showed himself to be powerful:

> *And Stephen, full of faith and power, did great wonders and miracles among the people.*
>
> Acts 6:8

As Stephen confronted the enemy and boldly confronted sin, he rubbed some people the wrong way. They were so infuriated by what he said that they quickly took up rocks and began to stone him to death:

> *And they stoned Stephen, calling upon God, and saying, Lord Jesus, receive my spirit. And he kneeled down, and cried with a loud voice, Lord, lay not this sin to their charge. And when he had said this, he fell asleep.* Acts 7:59-60

The amazing thing is that even while Stephen was being stoned, he received a special revelation of the nature of God:

> *But he, being full of the Holy Ghost, looked up*
> *stedfastly into heaven, and saw the glory of God,*
> *and Jesus standing on the right hand of God,*
> *and said, Behold, I see the heavens opened, and*
> *the Son of man standing on the right hand of*
> *God.* Acts 7:55-56

Stephen received a revelation of Yahweh, the Deliverer, the Rescuer. In many parts of the world you can see artistic interpretations of what men saw at various times. Usually, it will show Jesus seated at the Father's right hand. Stephen saw Him standing. That may not speak anything special to you, but it does to me. As Stephen was paying the ultimate price in persecution and betrayal, the Lord of Righteousness stood up for him. In the midst of your trial and tribulations, the Lord will stand up for you too. When you suffer persecution and betrayal, He will be there to comfort you. You just need to know Him. Then the One who is called Faithful and True will stand for you when you need Him.

There are, of course, many other names for God. These are just a few. Others are the King of Kings, the Lord of Lords, the Beginning and the End, the First and the Last, the Alpha and the Omega, the Root and the Offspring of David, the Bright and Morning Star, the Lion of the Tribe of Judah.

When Jesus was here on the earth, He was called the Logos (the Word), the Son of God, the Son of Man, the Son of David, the Lamb of God, the New Adam, Second Adam or Last Adam, the Light of the World, the King of the Jews, Rabboni and Rabbi. He is Jesus, and there is power in His name.

We are to baptize new believers in that precious name, signifying to the whole world that they are His:

> *Then Peter said unto them, Repent, and be baptized every one of you in the name of Jesus Christ for the remission of sins, and ye shall receive the gift of the Holy Ghost.*   Acts 2:38
> (see also Acts 8:16, 10:48 and 22:16)

Yes, there is power in His name. What about you? What are you waiting for? Begin to contend today for *His Light, His Power, His Presence, His Glory.*

Lord Jesus,

You are wonderful. You are wonderful in every way. You are a good and faithful God, a loving God, a forgiving God. You are the King of Glory. You're the King of Kings and Lord of Lords. You're the Beginning and You're the Ending. You're the First and Last. You're the Alpha and the Omega. You're the Root and Offspring of David. You're the Bright and Morning Star. You are the Lion of the Tribe of Judah. Come and roar in our midst. Roar in our hearts.

Wonderful Jesus, You see and know our hearts. I thank You, Lord, that You're a God who speaks to us. Declare Your purpose, Your will, Your calling to us in this season. Let Your Kingdom come. Let Your will be done in our lives. Let not one grain fall to the ground, but let the fullness of the harvest that You have ordained for us from the beginning of time come to pass. Give us fruit and fruit that lasts.

Father, consecrate us once again this day, that You would be first and foremost in our lives. And not just first, but that You alone would sit on the throne of our hearts.

Father, let Your hand of blessing, Your hand of favor, rest upon Your people. Father, bless them. Bless their families. Bless their homes. Bless them in their work. Bless them in their leisure. Bless them in their coming and going. Bless them physically, spiritually, emotionally and financially. Let Your blessings overtake them.

In Jesus' glorious name,
Amen!

THERE IS FREEDOM IN HIS NAME. HIS NAME GIVES US POWER TO SET CAPTIVES FREE, AND HIS NAME EMPOWERS THE CAPTIVES TO BE SET FREE AND TO REMAIN FREE!

Chapter 6

The Power of His Spirit

And Jesus returned in the power of the Spirit into Galilee: and there went out a fame of him through all the region round about.

Luke 4:14

The word *Shekinah*, referring to the visible glory of God, is a transliteration of a Hebrew word meaning "the one who dwells" or "that which dwells" and was used to describe the light on the Mercy Seat of the Ark of the Covenant kept in the Holy of Holies in the wilderness Tabernacle and later in the Temple in Jerusalem. My whole heart in this season is to establish a dwelling place for Him, for His Spirit, for His presence and for His power.

The Shekinah symbolizes the divine presence (see Exodus 25:8). The word *Shekinah* itself is only found in the Amplified Bible, but the root word *shakan* is found in all original manuscripts and means "to dwell, to settle down, to tabernacle with, to have a habitation" and the related word *mishkan* (tabernacle) are both frequently used and are both associated with the presence of God, His Spirit (and His glory) dwelling with man.

The meaning of the word *Shekinah* (the One Who dwells) reminds us that we did not seek to dwell with God, but He with us. This truth should evoke continual thanksgiving in all those who have been brought into covenant with Him under the shelter of His wings.

In Exodus, we see that it was God Who first expressed His a desire to dwell among men, instructing Moses to tell the people to construct a sanctuary for Him so that He might dwell (*shakan*) among them.

Though my relationship with the Heflin family ministry at Calvary Pentecostal Campground, I had the opportunity to experience and learn more about this Shekinah glory in a deeper way then I ever had before. I knew the moment I got there that I was in deeper waters.

The *Glory* series of books by Ruth Ward Heflin came alive in this heavenly atmosphere that was cultivated by the revelation she had received from

Psalm 100 of how to enter into the glory realm though praise and worship. The higher the praise and the deeper the worship, the greater the glory!

Then Pat Francis, a powerful apostolic leader from Toronto, Ontario, shared with me another dimension of God's presence, the *chayil*. According to *Strong's* #2428: *chayil* (pronounced ca heel) means "a force, whether of men, means or other resources; an army, wealth, virtue, valor, strength:—able, activity, (+) army, band of men (soldiers), company, (great) forces, goods, host, might, power, riches, strength, strong, substance, train, (+)valiant(-ly), valor, virtuous(-ly), war, worthy(-ily)."

In the *Brown-Driver-Briggs Hebrew Lexicon* we find that *chayil* means "strength, might, efficiency, wealth, army, ability, force, might ... valiant ... ." This was like the power that God gave to Gideon to make him a mighty man of valor. He looked at himself as weak and a failure, but God told him, *"Go in the strength that you have; am I not with you?"*

> *And the angel of the LORD appeared unto him [Gideon], and said unto him, The LORD is with thee, thou mighty man of valour.*
> *And Gideon said unto him, Oh my LORD, if the LORD be with us, why then is all this befallen*

us? and where be all his miracles which our fathers told us of, saying, Did not the LORD bring us up from Egypt? but now the LORD hath forsaken us, and delivered us into the hands of the Midianites.

And the LORD looked upon him, and said, Go in this thy might, and thou shalt save Israel from the hand of the Midianites: have not I sent thee? And he said unto him, Oh my LORD, wherewith shall I save Israel? behold, my family is poor in Manasseh, and I am the least in my father's house. And the LORD said unto him, Surely I will be with thee, and thou shalt smite the Midianites as one man. And he said unto him, If now I have found grace in thy sight, then shew me a sign that thou talkest with me. Judges 6:12-17

One of the finest verses in the Scriptures concerning the power of God is found in the Book of Acts. The power came when the Spirit came:

But ye shall receive power, after that the Holy Ghost is come upon you: and ye shall be witnesses unto me both in Jerusalem, and in all Judaea, and in Samaria, and unto the uttermost part of the earth. Acts 1:8

The Power of His Spirit

Chayil, glory, is the manifested power and glory of the Lord Jesus Christ, by His Spirit, in and through His servants. It is power to witness:

Jesus had the following conversation with His disciples:

> *And [Jesus], being assembled together with them, commanded them that they should not depart from Jerusalem, but wait for the promise of the Father, which, saith he, ye have heard of me. For John truly baptized with water; but ye shall be baptized with the Holy Ghost not many days hence.*
>
> *When they therefore were come together, they asked of him, saying, Lord, wilt thou at this time restore again the kingdom to Israel?*
>
> *And he said unto them, It is not for you to know the times or the seasons, which the Father hath put in his own power. But ye shall receive power, after that the Holy Ghost is come upon you: and ye shall be witnesses unto me both in Jerusalem, and in all Judaea, and in Samaria, and unto the uttermost part of the earth."*   Acts 1:5-8

When the Spirit fell upon the believers on the Day of Pentecost, they went right out and started to witness to others. The power of the Spirit is the power to save, heal, deliver and to overcome any enemy. God is practical, and He wants to empower us, giving us the power to win, the power to overcome. This is the power of His Holy Spirit!

The early believers prayed for the power to do signs, wonders and miracles:

> *Now, Lord, consider their threats and enable your servants to speak your word with great boldness. Stretch out your hand to heal and perform signs and wonders through the name of your holy servant Jesus.* Acts 4:29-30, NIV

When they prayed this prayer, even more of the power of the Spirit came upon them:

> *After they prayed, the place where they were meeting was shaken. And they were all filled with the Holy Spirit and spoke the word of God boldly.* Acts 4:31, NIV

The Spirit of the Lord was upon Jesus:

> *A shoot will come up from the stump of Jesse;*
> *from his roots a Branch will bear fruit.*

The Power of His Spirit

The Spirit of the Lord will rest on him —
   the Spirit of wisdom and of understanding,
   the Spirit of counsel and of might,
   the Spirit of the knowledge and fear of the
   Lord.   Isaiah 11:1-2, NIV

He is the Spirit of might, the Spirit of wisdom, the Spirit of counsel and the Spirit of a sound mind. We need Him and the gifts He imparts, the dreams and visions He gives, and we need Him to come with times of refreshing in His presence. This is the season were in, the restoration of all things, the biblical model of the emerging twenty-first-century end-time Church.

We are told that times of refreshing, revival, will come in the presence of the Lord, until the restoration of all things. And then the Lord will return:

> *Repent ye therefore, and be converted, that your sins may be blotted out, when the times of refreshing shall come from the presence of the Lord; and he shall send Jesus Christ, which before was preached unto you: whom the heaven must receive until the times of restitution of all things, which God hath spoken*

> *by the mouth of all his holy prophets since the*
> *world began.*   Acts 3:19-21

When I pray, I pray in the name of Jesus Christ, that name above every other name, but I also pray in the power of the Holy Spirit. He is the power force in the Earth today, and so we all need to know the power of the Holy Ghost.

We also need the gifts of the Spirit, and you can't have the gifts without the Spirit who gives them. You must first know the Spirit and develop a relationship with Him in order to receive the power He offers. This is power to personally overcome, and then it is power to change your world. This power of the Spirit is transforming. It transforms us, and it transforms others.

A key to gaining the power of God's Spirit is to be hungry for it. I was hungry twenty years ago, and I am still hungry today. In fact, as I have noted earlier, I'm hungrier now than ever before. I am totally dependent upon the power of God, the power to save, the power to heal and the power to deliver!

Paul wrote to the Roman believers:

> *I beseech you therefore, brethren, by the mercies*
> *of God, that you present your bodies a living*

*sacrifice, holy, and acceptable unto God, which
is your reasonable service.*   Romans 12:1

If you have been saved, I mean really saved, I'm talking about being so saved, then there is just one reasonable way to respond to the One who saved you. If Jesus actually came and saved your life, then there's only one proper response on your part, and that is to give yourself as a living sacrifice for Him.

Paul continued:

*And be not conformed to this world: but be ye
transformed by the renewing of your mind, that
ye may prove what is that good, and acceptable,
and perfect, will of God.*   Romans 12:2

We must not be conformed to this world, and we also must not be conformed to the church world. The church world would like for that religious spirit to come upon us and cause us to settle for less than God has prepared for us. We must be different. We must remain on the prophetic edge, willing to pay any price to see the power of God made real to those who are hungering and thirsting for it.

We need the power and presence of God's Spirit to win this war, to change ourselves and our circumstances and to change the world around us. We need His power to heal and His power to deliver. That power is waiting for us. So, what are you waiting for? Contend today for *His Light, His Power, His Presence, His Glory.*

> **Heavenly Father,**
>
> **Thank You for a fresh anointing, a fresh release of the power of Your Spirit in our lives, a fresh stirring of all the gifts and the power of Your Spirit.**
>
>

In Jesus' name,

Amen!

WE ALL NEED THE GIFTS OF THE SPIRIT, AND YOU CAN'T HAVE THE GIFTS WITHOUT THE SPIRIT WHO GIVES THEM!

Chapter 7

The Power of His Word

For the word of God is quick, and powerful, and sharper than any twoedged sword, piercing even to the dividing asunder of soul and spirit, and of the joints and marrow, and is a discerner of the thoughts and intents of the heart.

Hebrews 4:12

I was saved through the Word of God. No one preached to me. In fact, I didn't know a single person who was saved. I didn't even know what salvation was or what it meant to be born again. I had been raised Catholic, but I was not even a real Catholic. My parents were not good Catholics either; they were good heathens. So I lived life my own way until I eventually found myself in a place of desperation. In that moment, by His Spirit and by the power of His Word, God saved me.

The Power of His Word

When I was in the 5th grade, we had been required to pick a portion from the Bible to read to the whole class. I chose the 23rd Psalm and was called upon to read it aloud. That had been the last time I read anything from the Bible.

But now I was in a place of desperation in my life, and suddenly the presence of the Lord came into the room and began to melt my heart. I remembered that there was a small New Testament there somewhere in the mess of that house, a Saint Joseph's Catholic Version. I started hunting for it. I don't remember how long that New Testament had been there, but I had never read from it until then. I found it, gratefully picked it up, and began reading.

In those moments, I felt God's presence so strong that I began to weep. It had been years since I wept. I was beginning to experience God's love like I had never experienced it in my life, His love expressed through the power of His Word. I had a hard heart from doing violent sports, but that day I got saved reading Jesus' words to Nicodemus.

Jesus replied, "Very truly I tell you, no one can see the kingdom of God unless they are born again."

"How can someone be born when they are old?"
Nicodemus asked. "Surely they cannot enter
a second time into their mother's womb to be
born!"
Jesus answered, "Very truly I tell you, no one
can enter the kingdom of God unless they are
born of water and the Spirit. Flesh gives birth
to flesh, but the Spirit gives birth to spirit.
"You should not be surprised at my saying,
'You must be born again.' The wind blows
wherever it pleases. You hear its sound, but you
cannot tell where it comes from or where it is
going. So it is with everyone born of the Spirit."

John 3:3-8, NIV

There, in the quiet of my home, with no one else around, I was saved. Yes, there is power in God's Word.

I now started reading the Bible, but I didn't understand a lot of what I was reading, and I didn't have anyone to help me. Once in a while, however, a certain verse or verses or certain words suddenly seem to light up and mean something wonderful to me.

I still wasn't attending any church. I had kind of grown up on the streets. But I did understand power. When I saw that there was another baptism, a baptism of fire, a baptism of the Holy Ghost, a baptism of power, I was immediately interested. Power interested me. I knew that I needed power to win in life.

For the first sixty days or so of my new existence in Christ, there was an amazing amount of grace on my life. Everything was different. The sky was bluer than it had ever been before, and the grass was greener. Everything was new and fresh, but at the same time there was a war going on inside of me. God was dealing with the issues of my life.

God not only had the power to save; He also had the power to deliver. I had been struggling with drugs and alcohol and sins of all kinds, and I needed power if I was to survive this battle that was going on inside of me. Fortunately, I *knew* that I needed power, and I began to cry out to God for that power. I had seen in His Word that it was available. The result was that one day I stopped along the road, got out of my car and prostrated myself in prayer on the side of the road in my business suit. Within moments, the Lord sovereignly baptized me in the Holy Spirit, there alongside the road, with traffic passing by in both directions.

When I received the baptism of the Holy Spirit, I not only got the Holy Spirit; I got the Holy Spirit *and power*. From that moment on, I began to receive dreams and visions, and the gifts of the Spirit began to operate in me (even though I didn't know what they were at the time).

I didn't have a church to go to for help, but I began reading all that I could from the Word, and I believed everything I read. Therefore, I not only read it; I read it, and then I began to apply it to my everyday life.

The dreams and visions I began to receive were very real and very alive, and what I learned through them I applied to my personal and business life, and things began to turn around for me. If we are to win this war, we will need the power of God's Word.

We say that God is love, and He certainly is. But that's not all He's about. He also knows how to go to war and to take out any enemy. He is a man of war. Now that you and I are engaged in the great end-time battles, we need Him, His presence and His power as never before. That power is found in His Word.

The Church of the Lord Jesus Christ was birthed in power in the first century. It was built in power by the early apostles. At times, they were so severely persecuted that they were running for their lives. When it was necessary, they stood their ground in the power of the Spirit and prevailed. The Spirit on them gave them a holy boldness to face any challenge and win. This book is all about the power and the presence of God and about accessing that power to change and impact lives for Christ. That requires that we know the power of His Word.

As I said, no one led me to the Lord. He saved me sovereignly through His Word. Therefore, from the very first day of my Christian life, I have loved the Word. I got saved through reading John's gospel, where Jesus spoke to Nicodemus (John 3). I also love the opening words of John:

> *In the beginning was the Word, and the Word was with God, and the Word was God. The same was in the beginning with God. All things were made by him; and without him was not any thing made that was made. In him was life; and the life was the light of men.* John 1:1-4

The Word tells me that without faith I cannot please God and Romans tells me that *"faith cometh by hearing, and hearing by the word of God"* (Romans 10:17).

Speaking of spiritual warfare, Paul wrote to the Ephesians that it was to be conducted by *"the sword of the Spirit, which is the word of God"* (Ephesians 6:17). We are to fight with this weapon, for it is powerful.

155

The Word of God tries me, it stretches me, it works on me. God told Joshua that if he was looking for success in anything, he had to be *"strong and courageous"* (Joshua 1:7). Then, in verse 8, He said:

> *This book of the law shall not depart out of thy mouth; but thou shalt meditate therein day and night, that thou mayest observe to do according to all that is written therein: for then thou shalt make thy way prosperous, and then thou shalt have good success.*   Joshua 1:8, KJV

The book of the law refers to the *logos* Word, the written Word, but there is also the *rhema* word, one that jumps out at you and speaks to you right now. It somehow just comes alive in you and motivates you to do God's will. There is also the spoken Word, preached or testified and there is the prophetic word. This can come through others or by my own confession and profession of faith or by declaration and proclamation:

> *Hast thou commanded the morning since thy days; and caused the dayspring to know his place; that it might take hold of the ends of the earth, that the wicked might be shaken out of it?*   Job 38:12-13

The Power of His Word

The New International Version says it this way:

Have you ever given orders to the morning, or shown the dawn its place, that it might take the earth by the edges and shake the wicked out of it?

I declare the truth of the Word over myself in my daily covering prayer. I make proclamations, for instance, "I am healthy, wealthy and wise." "I am filled with the Holy Spirit and empowered to do the will and the work of the Lord, empowered with faith, hope, joy, patience, wisdom, courage and, most of all, the love of God." "I love the Lord, and His light shines in me. Therefore, the anointing in me is increasing every day."

God's Word has the power to always be new to us. There are many mysteries in His Word, and He delights to reveal them to us little by little. These mysteries are not hidden *from* us but, rather, hidden *for* us and for our children. And this is a season in which many of these mysteries are being revealed. Understanding God's Word will enable us to overcome and to do powerful things for His Kingdom.

God's Word is not, as some believe, a *mystical* Gospel. It is a very simple and very practical, so that we can all hear it and believe.

God is calling a simple people because simple people empowered by His Word can make a difference in this world. He doesn't call those who are wise in their own sight.

Do you love His Word? Do you believe what He says? Then, what are you waiting for? Start contending today for *His Light, His Power, His Presence, His Glory*.

Father,

I thank You for Your Word. There is power in it. I ask You now, in Jesus' name, that You would illuminate Your Word and use it to bring rhema guidance and direction to our lives. I pray for a Spirit of revelation, wisdom and understanding to be released to us in this moment and in this season, as we press in to You for more. Let Your Word come alive in our spirits.

In Jesus' name,
Amen!

GOD IS CALLING A SIMPLE PEOPLE BECAUSE SIMPLE PEOPLE EMPOWERED BY HIS WORD CAN MAKE A DIFFERENCE IN THIS WORLD!

Chapter 8

The Power of Unity

Behold, how good and how pleasant it is for brethren to dwell together in unity! It is like the precious ointment upon the head, that ran down upon the beard, even Aaron's beard: that went down to the skirts of his garments; as the dew of Hermon, and as the dew that descended upon the mountains of Zion: for there the LORD commanded the blessing, even life for evermore.

Psalm 133:1-3

There is power available to us as individuals, but there is much more power available to us when we join hands and unite hearts. There is nothing quite like the power of unity, the power of harmony, the power and togetherness among brothers.

The Power of Unity

When Fred and Val Bennett were with us in Pensacola for a marriage weekend, he said something that laid a foundation stone in my heart and life: "I want to be more one today then yesterday." He was talking about the power of unity in marriage, in covenant, about teamwork in ministry, business or life. On this subject, the Word of God declares:

> *Again I say unto you, That if two of you shall agree on earth as touching any thing that they shall ask, it shall be done for them of my Father which is in heaven. For where two or three are gathered together in my name, there am I in the midst of them.* Matthew 18:19-20

When we join hands with others, we are honoring the presence of the Lord in our midst through a spirit of unity and harmony. Whether it is a leadership team or a group of any kind, there is power in unity, the power of the multiplication of force.

The Bible tells us that one can put a thousand to flight, but joining forces with another causes us to put ten thousand to flight (see Deuteronomy 32:30). Wow! The power of unity is amazing. Adding just one other person can multiply our force ten times. That is powerful.

Think for a moment of a worship team of six or eight or ten and imagine what they might accomplish if they all came into true unity. They would have more than enough power over any demonic forces that opposed them. And that same truth applies to any group with any purpose.

It always starts with one, but the power of oneness is not the power of an individual, but rather the power of several or many individuals working in unity. In that place of unity, each one brings to the table their individuality, their particular giftings, talents and abilities, and no one is greater or higher than the others.

Each of us can only walk in the revelation we have, but when we walk in unity with others, there is a rare completeness. The knowledge of each one combined makes us all stronger. We are not *competing with* each other, but rather *completing* each other. We each bring our own thoughts, backgrounds and experiences to the table in unity, but Christ is also in our midst, and we have access to the mind of Christ, the great creative power of God.

If God is in our midst, and we are in unity with each other, God reveals Himself to us, not just through His wisdom and understanding (which is the most important element of revelation), but also through the information we have all gathered—whether through education, experience, research or relationship. No one person gets the glory, and this accumulation of revelation and information through unity opens to us all the mind of Christ.

I spend part of my year in Canada and part of it in Florida. After I was in Canada for a few months, my heart was touched when I read a post on The Dwelling Place web site which said, "Our pastors are coming home!" What an honor it was for me to hear our people in Pensacola call us "our pastors." As many know, that is not my root gift or calling, but I received their words as a term of endearment and respect. Each of us must operate, not according to title, background or intelligence, but through the heart of unity that is in Christ. That act on our part will bring the heart of Christ into every situation, circumstance and discussion.

I have a little different perspective on the role of a pastor than most. I honor and thank God for my pastor, but we, the people, do not exist for the pastor. This power is available to all. I exist as a pastor to serve my people and my God, by empowering and equipping His people to answer their call. It is not enough for them to watch *me* answer *my* call. God's Kingdom is an upside-down Kingdom. I exist to equip and serve His Body. I am here for them, not them for me.

This powerful principle is not based on title, office or calling. It is available to every believer, every couple, every ministry and business, every team. It's not the name on the back of the jersey that's important, but the name on the front. This is the power of one, the power of the team, the power of unity and harmony.

Where do we start? We start with our covenant relationships—our marriage and our church family—rallying around the vision of God, not around a man or a woman. We honor God in our midst and the revelation He gives, as we wrap our heart in unity around it.

Reach out to someone in your life, friends or family members, where you have allowed something to divide or separate you. Then quickly step back into unity. It can be just that easy. No two people agree about everything all the time. Therefore we have to choose to be in agreement so that we can access the power and blessing of unity.

When we are in unity, our problems are not even half as bad because we carry and share those burdens together. Our victories are twice as good because we have someone to celebrate them with.

No matter the trial or test, no matter how hot things get, Jesus said He would never leave us or forsake us.

Do you remember those three Hebrew boys who were thrown into the fire? Jesus appeared in their midst and kept them from the destruction of the flames, showing Himself faithful to them before King Nebuchadnezzar:

> *And these three men [Shadrach, Meshach, and Abed-Nego], firmly tied, fell into the blazing furnace. Then King Nebuchadnezzar leaped to his feet in amazement and asked his advisers, "Weren't there three men that we tied up and threw into the fire?"*
> *They replied, "Certainly, Your Majesty."*
> *He said, "Look! I see four men walking around in the fire, unbound and unharmed, and the fourth looks like a son of the gods."*
>
> Daniel 3:23-25, NIV

These three men were in unity. They would not be moved. They stood firm, agreed together and the Lord showed up for them.

I know that unity is not easy. It is never easy for a man or woman to lay their personal vision on the altar for the greater glory that comes in the corporate vision. It's never easy to lay down the desire to preach or teach and prophesy. I like the description of the living creatures. No matter what direction they moved in, it was always forward. When you agree with the corporate vision, it may seem like you're taking a step backward or sideways, but if it takes you to a place of unity, you can't lose. That will always carry you forward.

Right now, we're in a terrible mess here in North America, and it needs to be taken care of somehow. It cannot be rectified by the work of a man, the mind of a man or the word of a man We need the power that is to be found in God alone. We need His presence. We need the power of unity.

One of the things that the Scriptures show will happen in the end-times is a mighty Spirit of unity coming to the Body of Christ, breaking down all barriers. Oh, how we need that!

I have never seen more division than I am seeing right now here in North America. We are now in a place of desperation and that qualifies us for a miracle. God is ready to do that miracle, and He will do it by His power.

The power of unity will come upon the Body of Christ, and we will begin to command His blessing. This will bring down the barriers that separate us—

race, gender, denomination and all the other silliness that man has interjected. As these barriers fall, a new unity will be the result. The power of unity is the prelude to blessing. Get ready for it. If we contend for it, we will have *The Power and the Presence.*

Dear Jesus,

I declare Your prayer recorded in John 17:20-22 over all of us in the Body of Christ today:

"I do not pray for these alone, but also for those who will believe in Me through their word; that they all may be one, as You, Father, are in Me, and I in You; that they also may be one in Us, that the world may believe that You sent Me. And the glory which You gave Me I have given them, that they may be one just as We are one."

John 17:20-22, NKJV

Amen!

I HAVE NEVER SEEN MORE DIVISION THAN I AM SEEING RIGHT NOW HERE IN NORTH AMERICA. WE ARE NOW IN A PLACE OF DESPERATION AND THAT QUALIFIES US FOR A MIRACLE!

Chapter 9

The Power to Gain Wealth

This Book of the Law shall not depart from your mouth, but you shall meditate in it day and night, that you may observe to do according to all that is written in it. For then you will make your way prosperous, and then you will have good success.　　　Joshua 1:8, NKJV

As many of you already know, I am not what is commonly called a "prosperity preacher." However, I would never preach a poverty Gospel either. The true Gospel message is that God wants us to prosper as our soul prospers. He wants to bless us for the same purpose he blessed Abraham, and that was to be a blessing to others. God wants to bless us and prosper us, and He wants us to succeed. Therefore we can conclude that God wants us to prosper in balance and purpose as our soul prospers (see 3 John 1:2-4), so that we can be a blessing to others and extend and advance His Kingdom.

His Word declares:

> *And you shall remember the LORD your God, for it is He who gives you power to get wealth, that He may establish His covenant which He swore to your fathers, as it is this day. Then it shall be, if you by any means forget the LORD your God, and follow other gods, and serve them and worship them, I testify against you this day that you shall surely perish.*
>
> Deuteronomy 8:18-19, NKJV

God wants us to remember Him when we gain wealth, status, influence and success. He also wants us to recognize that He (and not we ourselves) is the One who gave us this ability. He also clearly lets us know why we are being blessed. It is because of the covenant He made with our forefathers. Our God is a covenant-making and a covenant-keeping God. As we have seen, His name is Faithful and True.

After having achieved a degree of success in business and sports and coming from a relatively poor background, sometimes people referred to me as a "self-made man." That was not true, and it is the last thing I would ever want people to think about me.

My heart is to be and to let others know that I am a God-made man. Before I knew Him, I had made a total mess of my life. He turned my mess into a miracle, and any success I've had can be attributed to Him, to His love, His mercy, His grace and His longsuffering in dealing with me and my ways. His ways are truly higher then our ways and his thoughts higher then our thoughts.

Many times, it seemed, God helped me to succeed in spite of myself. He is good all the time, and all the time He is good.

Prosperity in the Bible is always linked to giving, and there are four biblical systems for us to use in giving:

GIVING OUR TITHES

Will a man rob God? Yet ye have robbed me. But ye say, Wherein have we robbed thee? In tithes and offerings. Ye are cursed with a curse: for ye have robbed me, even this whole nation. Bring ye all the tithes into the storehouse, that there may be meat in mine house, and prove me now herewith, saith the LORD of hosts, if I will not open you the windows of heaven, and pour you out a blessing, that there shall not be room enough to receive it. And I will rebuke the devourer for your sakes, and he shall not destroy the fruits of your ground; neither shall your vine cast her fruit before the time in the field, saith the LORD of hosts. And all nations shall call you blessed: for ye shall be a delightsome land, saith the LORD of host.   Malachi 3:8-12

Mave and I and our ministry believe in tithing. Some people will state that it is an Old Testament model, but we believe that Jesus clearly confirmed it and even took it to a higher level in the New Covenant.

If you are looking for a New Testament model for giving, it is much more than ten percent. It is covenant stewardship. This means that everything that belongs to Jesus belongs to us, but it also means that everything that belongs to us belongs to Him. We are to be faithful stewards of everything He gives us.

When you give your tithe, God's promise is to break the curses off of your finances and open the windows of Heaven and pour out a blessing you won't be able to contain. Wow! Why wouldn't we tithe?

GIVING ALMS

Thou shalt surely give him, and thine heart shall not be grieved when thou givest unto him: because that for this thing the LORD thy God shall bless thee in all thy works, and in all that thou puttest thine hand unto. For the poor shall never cease out of the land: therefore I command thee, saying, Thou shalt open thine hand wide unto thy brother, to thy poor, and to thy needy, in thy land.

Deuteronomy 15:10-11

Cornelius, a Roman centurion, an officer of that famous army, got God's attention by sending a sweet scent up to Heaven with his alms (see Acts 10).

GIVING OUR FIRSTFRUITS

Honor the LORD with your possessions,
And with the firstfruits of all your increase;
So your barns will be filled with plenty,
And your vats will overflow with new wine.

Proverbs 3:9-10, NKJV

Whether I'm reaping or starting something new, I always want to make a firstfruits offering. God's promise is that my vats will then overflow with the new wine. If you're looking for the new wine in the new thing your doing, it is released when you offer God your firstfruits.

UNDERSTANDING SEEDTIME AND HARVEST

While the earth remaineth, seedtime and harvest, and cold and heat, and summer and winter, and day and night shall not cease.

Genesis 8:22

Once you get a revelation of seedtime and harvest, it will change your life. God has tied the spiritual laws with the natural laws, to let us know that this is a spiritual principal. It is part of a perpetual covenant that He made with Noah, and just as day and night, it will not end.

This principle not only applies to your finances, but also to every other area of your life. Once you understand the principle, you will want to turn everything in your life into seed and sow it into the Kingdom of God: your time, your energy, your creativity, your talent, your ability ... everything you have and everything you are.

We simply cannot out-give God. He cannot owe us anything. If you come to Him with a spoon, He will come to you with a shovel. If you come to Him with a shovel, He will come to you with a front-end loader. Test Him in this!

Remember: He is the Lord of the Harvest. His eye is on your seed because His heart is for your harvest.

An Isaiah 60 mandate is now coming upon the Church:

> *Arise, shine; for thy light is come, and the glory of the LORD is risen upon thee.*   Isaiah 60:1

God has promised:

- *"The LORD shall arise upon thee, and his glory shall be seen upon thee"* (verse 2).
- *"The Gentiles shall come to thy light, and kings to the brightness of thy rising"* (verse 3).
- *"Thy sons shall come from far, and thy daughters shall be nursed at thy side"* (verse 4).
- *"The abundance of the sea shall be converted unto thee"* (verse 5).
- *"The forces of the Gentiles shall come unto thee"* (verse 5).

- *"The multitude of camels shall cover thee, the dromedaries of Midian and Ephah"* (verse 6).
- *"All they from Sheba shall come: they shall bring gold and incense"* (verse 6).
- *"All the flocks of Kedar shall be gathered together unto thee"* (verse 7).
- *"The rams of Nebaioth shall minister unto thee"* (verse 7).
- *"They shall come up with acceptance on mine altar, and I will glorify the house of my glory"* (verse 7).

"Surely the isles shall wait for me, and the ships of Tarshish first, to bring thy sons from far, their silver and their gold with them, unto the name of the Lord thy God, and to the Holy One of Israel, because he hath glorified thee" (verse 9).

- *"And the sons of strangers shall build up thy walls"* (verse 10).
- *"And their kings shall minister unto thee"* (verse 10).
- *"Thy gates shall be open continually; they shall not be shut day nor night; that men may bring unto thee the forces of the Gentiles, and that their kings may be brought"* (verse 11).

God wants His people to be wealthy, and poverty

is definitely not a blessing from God. We must break off any poverty mentality that hinders us and realize that God wants to give us the power to gain wealth, so that we can be blessed and so that we can extend and advance His Kingdom.

There is available to us a special anointing for business. I know something about that because I was in business for many years.

When I got saved, I had never been in business before, but the Lord began to teach me about business. This is something the entire Body of Christ must learn, for there will come a serious transference of wealth in the days ahead, a business empowerment for the Body, an anointing for business, a release of the power to gain wealth. Kingdom wealth builders will soon emerge, and wonderful things will be released in the Body of Christ.

Some are saying that we need a return to the first-century Church, but I don't think so. God is preparing the twenty-first-century Church. This is the Church that will usher in the second coming of the Lord. This is the Church that will reap the great end-time harvest, a greater harvest than has ever been recorded in the history of the world. Consequently, we will do much more than that first-century Church ever did. In the first century, they needed the power to birth the Church, and now we need the power to finish the work. Included in that is the power to gain wealth. So, what are you waiting for? Begin to contend today for *His Light, His Power, His Presence, His Glory.*

Father,

I thank You that it is Your desire that we prosper even as our soul prospers. I thank You for the power to gain wealth, the anointing for business and pray that You would release this anointing now over us, Your people, to enter into the visionary realm. Release to us new creative ideas, concepts and strategies to birth, to build, to excel and to succeed. Give us dreams and vision and revelation knowledge to accomplish it all for Your glory.

In Jesus' mighty name,
Amen!.

ONCE YOU GET
A REVELATION
OF SEEDTIME
AND HARVEST,
IT WILL CHANGE
YOUR LIFE.
GOD HAS TIED
THE SPIRITUAL
LAWS WITH THE
NATURAL, TO
LET US KNOW
THAT THIS IS
A SPIRITUAL
PRINCIPAL!

Chapter 10

Born in the Power

Jesus replied, "You are in error because you do
not know the Scriptures or the power of God."
Matthew 22:29, NIV

I mentioned in Chapter 7 how I was saved by the
power of God's Word. Then, as I also noted in an earlier chapter, I found myself in a terrible battle. I had
received an exceedingly abundant grace, but there
was a very real war going on inside of me. About a
month and a half after being saved, I was crying out
for more of God's power because of the battle I was
in, and that was when He baptized me in the Holy
Ghost there on the side of the road. I began to speak
in a language I didn't understand.

Even as I spoke in this strange language, my heart
was crying out for an interpretation. I had come to

realize that I needed this baptism of fire, this baptism of power and had said to God, "Where is it? I need it if I'm to overcome."

It was then that the same presence that had come into my living room to save me now came into the car, and I begn to weep again, uncontrollably. I was weeping so hard that I decided to stop on the side of the road.

I'm not sure why, but I got out of the car, and the next thing I knew I was lying on my face on the side of the road, weeping. Then, suddenly, I heard myself speaking that strange language and had no idea what I was saying.

Then I heard my heart speaking to me, and through it, God was saying: "He is the King of Kings and He is the Lord of Lords. He is the Beginning and He is the Ending. He is the First and He is the Last. He is the Alpha and He is the Omega. He is the Root and Offspring of David. He is the Bright and Morning Star. He is the Lion of the Tribe of Judah."

I hadn't known any of that. I had only been saved a few weeks, and I had just started reading the Word in seriousness. But my spirit knew, and the Holy Spirit was bearing witness that Jesus was who He says He is. God was showing me that Jesus was seated at the right hand of the Father and that everything He said would indeed happen. So, from that day, all I did was believe, with the simplicity of my faith, what God was saying.

As I noted in Chapter 9, God then began to move in my life, giving me dreams and visions and teaching me about business. It was a very exciting time for me, and my faith grew in leaps and bounds.

Twenty years passed, and I was still serving the Lord and declaring His name, and I had a television program on which I would witness from time to time. The blunt truth, however, was that I had lost my edge. I had lost my first love. For all intents and purposes, I was backslidden. There is no other way to say it. I was now just going through the motions of religion and church life and had become a bit of a mocker.

I mocked what I was seeing in the church. "God," I said, "if I ran a business that You gave me the way these people run the church that You gave them, I would quickly be out of business." Thankfully, I quickly realized my need and began to cry out to God. There had to be more. Someone had to know about revival.

One day I passed a little church and noticed that they had something on their sign outside about revival. According to the sign, the revival was to begin at 7:00 that evening. I made it a point to attend. I needed revival.

I had never seen anything like what was happening in that little church. People were all over the floor. Some were laughing, some were crying, some were rolling around on the floor. Others were running around the room. It was all very strange to me. The next thing I knew I was on my face prostate on the floor.

I don't know how long I was down there, but when I got up I saw a man who was making the rounds, laying his hands on various ones and praying for them. He got to me and wanted to pray for me, but I didn't yet understand the laying on of hands. Still unchurched, I was ignorant of so much. To tell the truth, I was a little bit frightened of his intentions.

That night, after I got home, I was thanking God for what I had seen and experienced. Even though everything was so new to me, I knew that it was the power of God, and the power of God had always ministered to me. As I was crying out to God, He said to me, "Why didn't you let that man pray for you?"

I came up with all the reasons I could think of, but none of them made any sense. Eventually, the Lord said, "It was just your pride! Pride kept you from My blessing."

I went back to that little church the next night, and the next, and I kept going back. People were being slain in the Spirit, and wonderful things were happening, but, interestingly, nothing else seemed to be happening to me. I was like a refrigerator, just standing there. But every day my hunger increased, and God's Word began to come alive to me, and my prayer life came alive all over again as well. So even though I didn't go down in the Spirit, the Spirit of God was working on me, and I was changing.

Before long I heard that real revival was taking place in a church in Pensacola, Florida. Some of the members of that little church had started traveling to Florida to experience the revival. When I heard about it, I got very excited. I was making something of a comeback, but the fight I had long experienced in my personal life continued. I knew that I needed more of the power of God. I wished that I could attend that revival.

One morning, at about 6:30, I was sitting at my desk, and I said to myself, "Man, I really would like to go there, but I have a couple of TV interviews this week, and I have business appointments scheduled." I listed every other reason I could think of why I couldn't go.

By 8:30, my service team members had all gone off to their assigned duties, and suddenly my secretary came in with the messages of the day. As I reviewed them, I was shocked to discover that every appointment scheduled for that week (seven of them in all) had cancelled. Every single one of them. This had never happened before.

As I was staring at the messages my secretary had placed on my desk, I heard the Lord, as plain as I have ever heard anyone. He said "Okay, big shot, what are you going to do now?" I picked up the phone, called my travel agent, and booked a flight to Pensacola.

I didn't know anyone in Pensacola, and I didn't know those from the little local church who were planning to go to the revival, so I decided to go on my own accord and get my own car and room, etc.

When the day came and I boarded the plane, I found that I was seated in the middle of the group from the little church. When I got to the hotel I had booked independently of them, they were all around me. When I got to the church the next morning and got in line, they were there as well. We were all so hungry.

We had heard about the crowds and the waiting lines at Brownsville Assembly of God Church, but it had seemed hard to believe at the time. But here we were now standing in line at about 8 o'clock in the morning, waiting for the 7 o'clock service that night. People were lined up under umbrellas, and we had to fend for ourselves for lunch.

Once the doors opened and seating was available that evening, it took just minutes to fill the building. It was all because of the amazing hunger for the presence and the power of God that was being demonstrated in that place every night. This was indeed a great move of God's Spirit.

The church in Brownsville was housed in a beautiful building, they had a beautiful choir, a great worship leader, Lindell Cooley, and a great evangelist, Steve Hill. Steve's preaching was very simple, but it had a great anointing upon it.

Many things caught my attention during that first service. For one, all of the young people ran to the front of the church and began dancing before the Lord as the song service got underway. I surely wasn't used to seeing that in church.

Another of the notable things was a lady in the choir whose head continually twitched or jerked from side to side. After she had done that for two and a half to three hours, I wondered how she could even think straight. That had to be the work of the

Holy Spirit. Other people were shaking, dancing and falling in the Spirit. For some reason, she stood out to me.

When a simple altar call was given that night, a young girl, perhaps fifteen years old, sang "Running to the Mercy Seat," and thousands of people streamed down to the altar to be prayed for. It was an awesome sight.

When I got back to my room that night, I thanked God for what I had seen and pondered its power. I had never seen anything like it before. The Lord said to me, "Why didn't you go forward?"

I was stunned and tried to offer excuses, "Well, I'm okay, and I've been okay for a while now." But I knew that God was dealing with me and soon found myself again on my face before Him.

It was as if a movie screen had appeared, and I saw myself in scenes from my life. In one scene, I was harboring unforgiveness in my heart against another person. In another, I had allowed a small sin to creep into my life. It wasn't much, but sin is a slippery slope. The next night, I answered the altar call, and I did it again the next night and the next. And I never stopped answering that call to get closer to God.

After praying in the altar for a while that first night, I went back to the book table to see what good books, tapes and videos they had for sale. And I've made that a habit ever since. There is so much to be learned, and we must learn it any and every way we can. Anointed books, CDs and DVDs are life-changing.

That night I said to the lady in charge of the book table, "I need some awesome teaching materials."

She pointed to a video and said, "This is for you, mister." It was a teaching on the life of an eagle.

I said, "Yeah, that's fine. I'll take it." But I was thinking to myself, "Yeah, sure, that's for me?" What the woman didn't know was that I had been saved through reading St. John's Gospel, often associated with the eagle, and subsequently, God had spoken to me to name my companies Eagle Systems, Eagle Monitoring, Eagle Security and Eagle Construction. I hadn't realized at the time that the eagle was the symbol of the office of the prophet and of prophecy.

I paid for the video, put it in my bag and took it back to my room. As soon as I could, I put on the video. It spoke of the joy of the mother eagle and how she was stirring up her nest, and as I listened to it, God called me to the ministry. He was calling me to sell my business, leave my home area and move to Pensacola to be part of the revival. I did it because I was so hungry for God's power.

Before long, I met Lila Terhune and began learning about true intercession. Until that time, I hadn't known what intercession was. Soon I discovered that this was my primary gifting. To some, that doesn't sound very exciting, but every true prophet, before they become a prophet, must become an intercessor. The same is true for pastors. You cannot be a five-fold minister without being an intercessor first. You must have a heart to pray, to intercede, to stand in the gap, to make up the hedge. God is bringing His prayer warriors to the forefront.

While I was studying with Lila Terhune, I met the lady who had drawn my attention that first night as she stood in the choir. She was a school teacher, had been in an accident, and, in the early days of the revival, had received her healing. Since then, every time she got in the presence of God, her head would shake uncontrollably for hours. That sign had ministered to me.

Any and every sign, wonder and miracle ministered to me. The gifts of the Spirit ministered to me. The fact that the lady at the book table had been prophetic enough to give me that video about the eagle and sense that I needed it ministered to me. It was the very video God used to call me to leave my business, leave my home, sell my property, and move all the way to Pensacola to attend the Bible School, when I knew no one in Pensacola. Wasn't I too old to attend Bible School?

I spent three years at Brownsville, and when I left I thought I was then going to start my own ministry. Instead, the Lord sent me to Calvary Campground in Ashland, Virginia, to sit for some months under the prophetic ministry of Ruth Ward Heflin and Sister Jane Lowder.

Ashland was different from Brownsville. In Brownsville, people were coming from all over the world, and there was a special anointing for salvation. The camp had more of a prophetic anointing. People were coming there for a very different reason. There the gifts of the Spirit were in operation, and signs and wonders were seen in every service. Gold dust was appearing on the believers, and oil flowed from their hands. In that atmosphere, my own gifts began to mature.

After those months in Ashland, God sent me to Canada to start a work, and I was determined to do it in His power. Eagle Worldwide Ministries, Eagle Worldwide Retreat and Revival Centre, Eagle Worldwide Network, the International Coalition of Prophetic Leaders and The King's Way in Hamilton, Ontario are all a result of that vision.

Born in the Power

I was originally drawn to those two places, Brownsville and Ashland, because of the power of God that was evident there, and I brought this same mentality into our ministry. So now we cannot afford to have less power today. We must move on to even greater depths of God's power. We must believe for the power, go where the power is being demonstrated and contend for the power in our own personal lives and ministries.

This end-time move of God's Spirit will be a move of signs, wonders and miracles. It has to be so that men will not take credit for it and say, "My program, my ministry or my teaching brought this about." It will be Christ and Christ alone. It will happen only by the power of God's Spirit. It will take nothing less to turn our nations right-side up and turn our churches right-side up. It will happen with us as it did with the early Church. Oh, how we need the Shekinah glory, the *cabod*, the heaviness of God's wonderful presence and power.

My whole heart in this season is to establish a dwelling place for the Lord, a dwelling place for His presence and His power. In keeping with that desire, The Dwelling Place is the name of our church in Pensacola, the apostolic center we were led to birth there in recent years. The Dwelling Place is indeed a dwelling place for God's presence and His power, a place where we can welcome Him, celebrate Him and experience Him in all of His glory. It is a place where torchbearers can come to light their fire and then take it back to the nations of the world.

In the Dwelling Place, we have keepers of the flame, intercessors who know God, know His voice and know His will, and we have true worshipers, those who know how to cultivate His presence.

When God sent me to Calvary Campground, I was able to read Ruth Heflin's now famous book *Glory*,[1] but I was also able to experience what I was reading. Sister Ruth had a powerful revelation about how to go about accessing the glory, and even though it was very simple, it worked. As we praised God until the Spirit of worship came, worshiped until the glory came and then stood in the glory, signs and wonders began to manifest. And the higher our praise went and the deeper our worship went, the greater the glory we saw and experienced.

The people of Calvary Campground not only had a revelation of God's presence; they were walking in it and living in it every hour of every day. For example, they did not get their musicians and worship leaders together to practice the music for a given

1, Hagerstown, MD, McDougal Publishing: 1990

service (as is common now in most churches). They just sang and played the music as it came to them, as God inspired them, but the point was that they genuinely praised God and genuinely worshiped Him, and they did it until His presence was manifested in their midst.

When we insist on the importance of seeing God's power manifest, some accuse us of seeking the Lord's hand and not His face. That is the furthest thing from the truth. We seek Him in praise and worship. We not only seek His face; we seek His heart. But His hand is part of His presence too, so we *do* seek His hand.

One night I was praying, and I said to God, "I am not seeking Your hand; I seek Your face." Later that night, I was praying for some provision that we needed for the ministry, and God showed me that I was indeed looking for His hand. In fact, I was looking for His right hand of power, His hand of provision. As I was crying out to Him, I heard Him say very clearly, "Oh, I thought you were not interested in My hand."

He was right. I didn't just need His face; I needed His hand; I needed all of Him. I needed provision for the vision He had given me through revelation, and I'm sure you have had that same experience. But He is the One who gives us the power to gain wealth, and it doesn't matter which part of Him we get that from. We will give Him all the glory for it and use it wisely for Kingdom purposes, to extend and advance His plan. This is what Kingdom wealth builders are meant to do.

I wanted more than His face, and I got it. And now I'm not willing to settle for anything less. His presence is not enough for me. I want to see His power as well. I need His power to overcome. I need His power to be successful in all that I do for Him. I need His power to win the battle that rages in our flesh. I cannot do the work He has assigned to me in the flesh. His Word is very clear:

> *Trust in the LORD with all thine heart; and lean not unto thine own understanding.*
> *In all thy ways acknowledge him, and he shall direct thy paths.*   Proverbs 3:5-6

I never want to be guilty of leaning on my own understanding. Instead, I want to always lean on the power of God, the gifts of God, the call of God on my life, the grace gift that He's given me, the anointing of His Spirit, the enduement of power from on high that He has so graciously imparted so that we can work in the supernatural, not the natural.

What made Azusa Street stand out was not the fancy preaching to be heard. It was the demonstration of the power of God that took place in those humble surroundings. What has kept Calvary Campground at the center of God's outpouring now for more than sixty years has been the simplicity of the presentation accompanied by the power of God's Spirit. That simplicity has turned countless average men and women into mighty warriors for the Kingdom.

Are you determined to be a flame for God in the days ahead? Then it's time to contend for *His Light, His Power, His Presence, His Glory.*

Father
I pray for a fresh release of Your power in the lives of my brothers and sisters today. Lord, that You would impart the gift of miracles and the gift of faith into their lives, that they would walk in the supernatural realm and that signs, wonders and miracles would follow them. Let them heal the sick, set the captives free, bind up the broken-hearted and give testimony of You, the only true and living God. That is the power of prophecy.   In Jesus' name,
Amen!

WHAT MADE AZUSA STREET STAND OUT WAS NOT THE FANCY PREACHING TO BE HEARD. IT WAS THE DEMONSTRATION OF THE POWER OF GOD THAT TOOK PLACE IN THOSE HUMBLE SURROUNDINGS!

Chapter 11

Go in the Strength You Have

The LORD turned to him [Gideon] and said, "Go in the strength you have and save Israel out of Midian's hand. Am I not sending you?"
                                        Judges 6:14, NIV

I mentioned Gideon earlier in the book, but I must give his amazing story more space. One of the early judges over Israel and a very respected military leader, Gideon was not always so powerful. As a young man, he had a serous problem. His problem was that he didn't believe in himself. He looked at himself as being weak and a failure. But, amazingly, God told him, *"Go in the strength you have."* Wow! God saw Gideon very differently than he saw himself.

Many times, you and I look at our enemies as did the men who were sent by Moses to spy out the land of

Canaan. They knew the promise of God, and they saw that it was a land flowing with milk and honey. They saw its amazing fruit. BUT they also saw how big the enemies were and how small they themselves looked in their own eyes. Sometimes we let our problems, situations, trials, tribulations and persecution seem very big in our own sight and look at ourselves as being so small. God is trying to give us another look.

The story of Gideon begins with the news that the tribal bands of marauders known as the Midianites had overrun the land, stolen everything that was worth taking and left the Israelites in great hardship. Gideon was wondering how he would feed his family. Then, in this time of severe distress, God came to speak to him:

> *And the angel of the LORD appeared unto him [Gideon], and said unto him, The LORD is with thee, thou mighty man of valour. And Gideon said unto him, Oh my LORD, if the LORD is with us, why then is all this befallen us? and where be all his miracles which our fathers told us of, saying, Did not the LORD bring us up from Egypt? but now the LORD hath forsaken us, and delivered us into the hands of the Midianites.*

> Judges 6:12-13

Have you ever felt like that? Have you ever said, "God, if You're really *with* me, why is all of this 'stuff' happening?" Most of us have. In a very real sense, Gideon was just sharing his heart with the Lord. Clearly he had heard stories from his forefathers of the miracles God had done to deliver them from Egypt. But where was God now? It seemed like a legitimate question.

It was in this moment that the Lord spoke those amazing words: *"Go in this thy might, and thou shalt save Israel from the hand of the Midianites: have not I sent thee?"* What? Did that even make sense?

It didn't make sense to Gideon. He objected that he was from the weakest tribe and he personally was one of the weakest members in that weak tribe. So how could all of this really happen? But God told him to go in the strength he had. Clearly that wasn't enough, but if Gideon obeyed, then God would strengthen him, and he would go in the power of God. *"Didn't I send you?"* If God sends us, then we can do whatever He commands, for He will also empower us.

Over the past three or four years, I, like many who are on the prophetic edge of what God is doing, have gone through many trials. At times, I have to admit, I was thinking, "God, why am I going through all of this? What's this about? Where is Your miracle-working power? Where are all the things we have been taught?" We are all human and we go through these moments. And yet God is saying, "Go in the strength you have, and I will do wonders for you!"

About five years ago now, I was diagnosed with stage-four lymphoma and had to go through a lot of treatments. Later, I had to undergo a second round of treatments. In the midst of all of that, the Lord, despite my weakness, would still open doors for me to travel and minister in other places. When these invitations came, I was hesitant. I felt so weak. How could I go? I remembered His words to Gideon, *"Go in this thy strength. Have not I sent you?"* Those words sustained me. If God said it, He will do it.

I want to always be a sent one, not just one who shows up. When I am sent, I can go, even in my weakness, and He will show Himself strong on my behalf. In some of my weakest moments, I have found the power and presence of God to be most real in my life. On a personal level and also on a corporate level, I have seen His power released in the midst of weakness.

There are times when you simply cannot look at what's on the surface. You have to know that God sent you and that His hand is upon you. You must hear His voice, "Go in the strength you have."

God said more to Gideon:

> *And the LORD said unto him, Surely I will be with thee, and thou shalt smite the Midianites as one man.* Judges 6:16

Wow! That just seemed too good to be true. Gideon asked God for a sign. Sometimes we're afraid to do that. Surely God will be angry with us if we ask Him for a sign. But He was not angry with Gideon and showed him the sign he had asked for.

Oh, beloved, right now, more than ever before, I'm so hungry and I must press into the heart of God for signs, wonders and miracles, for gifts in the power of the Holy Spirit. This is the power of God made manifest, made real, so that people can taste it and drink it in. That's why people come to our churches from all over the world. They don't just come to hear good preaching or good worship or good music. They come to taste the power and the presence of the living God. They come to see the gifts of the Spirit in operation, the life-changing power of prophecy released.

Yes, they want to hear the Word of the Lord, and that Word will change their minds and hearts. But primarily they come for the power of God! They don't come for a person, and they don't come for a vacation. They don't spend six month's salary to travel halfway around the world, from India or Africa, just to be entertained. They are coming to taste the power and the presence of Almighty God!

Just as the Lord said, Gideon went on to defeat the feared Midianites and to become a great leader in Israel, and you can do what God has called you to do. How? By faith. We prophesy according to our faith (see Romans 12:6), we do miracles and bring healing the sick by faith, and we cast out demons by faith. But we cannot do it alone. It is imperative that we recognize that God is with us and that He has commissioned us to do His work.

Yes, the Hope of Glory dwells within us, and the power that raised Jesus Christ from the dead is active in our lives too.

We have the power of Almighty God. Jesus said:

All power is given unto me in heaven and in earth. Matthew 28:18

So, He had all power. Then, however, He made a startling statement:

> *Go ye therefore, and teach all nations, baptizing them in the name of the Father, and of the Son, and of the Holy Ghost: teaching them to observe all things whatsoever I have commanded you: and, lo, I am with you always, even unto the end of the world. Amen.*
>
> Matthew 28:19-20

With those words, Jesus transferred His power and authority to us, and commissioned us to go and do the same works He had done while on the Earth. The power still resides in Him, but we have full access to that power. It is time to activate our faith and start doing the works of God.

Many times, when I am about to pray for a person, I don't necessarily have a word for them in that moment. I begin to minister to them by faith, and the word they need comes to me. The anointing brings what we need in the moment we need it.

Only one of the gifts of the Spirit is called the gift of faith, but every single one of them operate by faith. What do I mean by that? I mean that you need enough faith to touch the heart of God, and He does the rest.

During the time of Moses' leadership of the people of Israel, Joshua was always in the background. He was known as Moses' faithful servant, and he may have conveyed Moses' messages to people at times. He was not the leader of the people, but then Moses died, and suddenly there was a vacuum of leadership. Or so everyone thought. In reality, God knew that He had His man. He said to Joshua:

> *Moses my servant is dead; now therefore arise, go over this Jordan, thou, and all this people, unto the land which I do give to them, even to the children of Israel. Every place that the sole of your foot shall tread upon, that have I given unto you, as I said unto Moses. From the wilderness and this Lebanon even unto the great river, the river Euphrates, all the land of the Hittites, and unto the great sea toward the going down of the sun, shall be your coast. There shall not any man be able to stand before thee all the days of thy life: as I was with Moses, so I will be with thee: I will not fail thee, nor forsake thee.* Joshua 1:2-5

So, there was no doubt in God's mind, but can we say the same for Joshua? In the next two verses,

God told him twice: *"Be strong and of a good courage"* (Joshua 1:6). *"Only be thou strong and very courageous"* (Joshua 1:7). God was ready to use Joshua as He had Moses, but Joshua had to believe in order to activate that power and claim his position of leadership.

Gideon would have to do the same. He could defeat the Midianites and all the other Ites if he contended for the same power of God that Moses and Joshua had tapped into. Thankfully, he did, and the rest is history. Oh, may we have a fresh baptism of power today so that we can lead God's people forward in the days to come. These are the days of refreshing. Take advantage of them to get yourself ready for battle.

When that glory descended upon the Upper Room in Jerusalem and that motley group of fishermen and tax collectors were filled with the Spirit, they went out and immediately began to do the work of the Kingdom. This same thing will happen to us, as darkness overtakes the earth and gross darkness the people. The glory of the Lord will come upon us and His power will be released through us.

How can you get ready for what lies ahead? Start spending more time in God's presence. Start filling your heart with His promises. Start contending for the faith once delivered to the saints. Get hungry for God and go after Him.

There is a guaranteed blessing for all those who are hungry. Ask God to make you more hungry today, and then don't be surprised when trials and tests come your way. Don't be surprised if desperation overtakes you. In your desperation, you will come to know better the God of all power.

What are you waiting for? Contend today for *His Light, His Power, His Presence, His Glory.*

Father,

Thank You for the Spirit of might, energy, strength and power to overcome our enemies and our own weaknesses and shortcomings. I bind every spirit of fear and insecurity in Jesus' name and pray that we would see ourselves though Your eyes. Raise us up in the confidence that we have in You. We know in our hearts that You will go with us, and we can do all things in and through You. We will give You all the glory, all the honor and all the praise.

In Jesus' name,
Amen!

JESUS TRANSFERRED HIS POWER AND AUTHORITY TO US AND COMMISSIONED US TO GO AND DO THE SAME WORKS HE HAD DONE WHILE ON THE EARTH!

Chapter 12

The Tribe of Hungry

Jesus entered Jericho and was passing through. A man was there by the name of Zacchaeus; he was a chief tax collector and was wealthy. He wanted to see who Jesus was, but because he was short he could not see over the crowd. So he ran ahead and climbed a sycamore-fig tree to see him, since Jesus was coming that way.

Luke 19:1-4, NIV

Zacchaeus is one of my favorite Bible characters. He was from my tribe, the tribe of Hungry. He was a rich man, but he was also small, and that seemed to give him a complex of sorts. To his credit, he wanted to see Jesus so badly that he climbed up into a tree, casting off all dignity and not worrying about what people might say. Are you that hungry to see the Lord today?

You should be. Nothing else will change our nations, only the presence and the power of God Himself.

The story continues:

> *When Jesus reached the spot, he looked up and said to him, "Zacchaeus, come down immediately. I must stay at your house today." So he came down at once and welcomed him gladly. All the people saw this and began to mutter, "He has gone to be the guest of a sinner." But Zacchaeus stood up and said to the Lord, "Look, Lord! Here and now I give half of my possessions to the poor, and if I have cheated anybody out of anything, I will pay back four times the amount." Jesus said to him, "Today salvation has come to this house, because this man, too, is a son of Abraham. For the Son of Man came to seek and to save the lost."* Luke 19:5-9, NIV

Did Zacchaeus put himself in danger climbing up that tree? Did he perhaps tear his fine clothing or dirty himself? If so, it didn't matter. All he could think about in that moment was that Jesus was coming and he had heard great things about Jesus and wanted to see Him and know Him.

This act spoke to Jesus, for as He came along that way, He suddenly stopped and looked up into that exact tree. Something had gotten His attention. There were many trees and many people milling about along the route, but Jesus stopped, looked up at this particular man this particular tree nand spoke to him: *"Zacchaeus, come down immediately. I must stay at your house today."*

This raises a lot of questions. How did Jesus know Zacchaeus' name? Why did He single him out of the crowd? Was it unusual for Him to invite Himself to someone's house to spend the night? Whatever the case, Jesus was going to Zacchaeus' house.

Zacchaeus was delighted, but I wonder if some of us would be. Would we think our house was too humble to receive the Lord of Lords? Would we worry that we could not entertain Him well enough? Jesus didn't consider staying in any other home. He goes where people are hungry for Him.

Zacchaeus was not a perfect man. Others knew it and criticized Jesus for going to the house of a sinner. The fact that he was a sinner suddenly dawned on Zacchaeus too (as happens in the Lord's presence), and he vowed to make right any wrong he had committed. Jesus responded, *"Today salvation has come to this house."*

The Tribe of Hungry

You and I need to become so hungry for God, for His presence and for His power that we place a demand on the anointing of God, just like the woman with the issue of blood who touched Jesus with her faith and hunger. Hunger and faith put a demand on the anointing that day. Jesus felt the virtue, the goodness, the anointing going forth from Him, and the woman was healed.

Before Jesus went back to Heaven, He instructed His disciples:

> *And, behold, I send the promise of my Father upon you: but tarry ye in the city of Jerusalem, until ye be endued with power from on high.*
>
> Luke 24:49

How long were they to tarry? It was indefinite. *"Tarry until ..."* These people had families, they had responsibilities, and yet they stayed right there and waited until the Spirit came upon them on the Day of Pentecost. What does it mean? It means that they were hungry for more of God. Some of them had walked with Jesus, eaten with Him, listened to His teachings. Others of them had felt His touch and been healed or delivered by Him. Whatever the case, they all wanted more, and they stayed there until more came.

Like the prophets of old, build an altar in your heart and then host God's presence and power. Build such altars in your place of business, in your school, in your factory. Let there come a circumcision of your heart, and then let it be a place where God is always welcomed and where He can abide.

Jesus knew what His disciples needed, and it was power, the power of the Holy Ghost, power to witness, power to change situations. He told them to wait in the Upper Room until they had it.

When John the Baptist was at the height of his notoriety, he made this statement:

> *I indeed baptize you with water unto repentance. but he that cometh after me is mightier than I, whose shoes I am not worthy to bear: he shall baptize you with the Holy Ghost, and with fire.* Matthew 3:11

Some were satisfied with John's baptism in water, but others contended for more, for the Greater One who would come and for the baptism with the Holy Ghost and fire He would bring. How about you? Are you hungry for more of God, hungry for more of His power and His presence?

The Tribe of Hungry

The humble disciples of Jesus would be required to build the Church from nothing. They started with one hundred and twenty no-name people. There were only Hebrews in that Upper Room. There wasn't a single Gentile among them. How, then, could they turn nations around and turn the world upside down? There wasn't a single theologian among them. They were fishermen and tax collectors. Just like you and me, they were just regular people. It was the unction of the Holy Spirit that came upon them and gave them the power to birth and to build the first-century Church. And we need that same power today in the twenty-first century, to bring in the greatest harvest known to man. We need that power to overcome the enemy and stand before God victorious.

As I have noted, God is practical, and He wants to empower us, thus enabling us to win, to overcome, and this can be done only through the power of the Holy Spirit. Are you hungry for more of God?

When I went to Calvary Campground that first time, there was something else I saw right away that I desperately wanted. I saw people who were able to work all day long, serving those who came, then in the evening they could be seen on the platform, praising and worshiping, and then ministering around the altars until very late at night.

They would be up early the next morning for prayer and more work, and they did this day in and day out for more than ten weeks each summer. They attended three services a day, plus did many other assigned tasks. They often got no breaks at all. It didn't take me long to say to one of the sisters, "There's a power here that I don't have, and it's a power that I need. What is it?" I was hungry for that power.

She said, "It's the power of might" and pointed me to Isaiah 11:1-2. That was the same Spirit that had been on Jesus Himself. (Incidentally, of the seven people who most influenced me in those days, five of them were women. I thought that was remarkable.) I sought God until I was satisfied that I had received what she was talking about. I will tell you more about it in my conclusions. Are you ready to contend for *His Light, His Power, His Presence, His Glory*?

Father,

I am believing You for an anointing of power to heal the sick and cast out demons. Your power enables us to do the greater works. It is the power to make a difference, the power to win, the power to overcome

obstacles and influences in our lives. I be-lieve in Your power, for I am a product of that power, a product of the laying on of hands. I believe in the doctrine of the laying on of hands. I believe in the power of the spoken Word and in its declaration. I be-lieve that it can happen and that it comes from that impartation. Let it be!

In Jesus' name,
Amen!

JESUS KNEW WHAT HIS DISCIPLES NEEDED, AND IT WAS POWER, THE POWER OF THE HOLY GHOST, POWER TO WITNESS, POWER TO CHANGE SITUATIONS!

Chapter 13

The Power to Win

And there shall come forth a rod out of the stem of Jesse, and a Branch shall grow out of his roots: and the spirit of the Lord shall rest upon him, the spirit of wisdom and understanding, the spirit of counsel and might, the spirit of knowledge and of the fear of the Lord.

Isaiah 11:1-2

This was what the passage she gave me that day said. It happened to Jesus, but when the same Spirit that came upon Jesus comes upon you, the result will be the same: wisdom, understanding, counsel and might, knowledge and the fear of the Lord.

When Jesus' mother asked Him about the wine for the feast, He answered that is was not yet His time. But somehow Mary knew better. Then suddenly the

Spirit came upon Jesus, and He turned water into wine. From that moment, He didn't just do a few miracles. Everything He did was miraculous! The Spirit of the Lord had come upon Him when He was baptized by John, but now He was being anointed for service. And God will do the same for you. A fresh anointing of fire will come upon you if you're hungry for it and contend for it.

At this moment, you may be going through trials and tribulations, but when you get into the presence the Lord, He will quickly recharge your batteries. No matter what is going on and no matter how you might feel, just get into His presence, and He will give you power to overcome it all. As you come into the presence of the Lord with praise and worship, His power will come upon you to bring you a time of refreshing. And immediately you will experience wisdom, counsel and the fear of the Lord.

One of the reasons sin is so rampant in the Body of Christ today is that we no longer have a healthy fear of the Lord. When the Spirit of the Lord comes upon us in seasons of refreshing, one of the results will be a renewed fear of God. This means that we can again reverence God. It doesn't mean we are afraid of Him. It means that we revere Him!

Peter wrote to the churches:

The Power to Win

And he shall send Jesus Christ which before was preached unto you: whom the heavens must receive until the times of restitution of all things, which God hath spoken by the mouth of all his holy prophets since the world began.

Acts 3:20-21

This is the season we are in right now. If anyone asks you what season we're in, tell them that it is the season of the restoration of all things. Everything that was lost over the centuries is being restored in preparation for the second coming of Christ. God is restoring the five-fold ministry, and He is restoring the gifts and their power to the Body. He is restoring all that was stolen. When all things have been restored, we will then see Jesus coming back again.

How can the restoration of all things come about? It can only come through a refreshing of the power and the presence of the Lord.

Far too many people are running away from church these days. We need something to draw them back, and the only thing that can do this is the power and the presence of God. I hear people preaching against the church, and when I hear that, I want to correct them. Our Lord is madly in love with His Church. Don't you be guilty of speaking against her.

Yes, we have problems in the church, but that does not change God's love for His Church. He loves the Church, and we are that Church.

Your denomination is not "the Church." Your fellowship is not "the Church." Your building is not "the Church." We, God's children, are the Church. Find all of those who are running away from the Church and tell them about God's season of refreshing. Encourage them to come back so that they can experience the power and the presence of the Lord, so that He can then restore to them all things. He is restoring the power and restoring the glory back to the Church so that we can all do the greater works He spoke of in John 14:

> *Verily, verily, I say unto you, He that believeth on me, the works that I do shall he do also; and greater works than these shall he do; because I go unto my Father.* John 14:12

You and I must divorce ourselves from the politics of the church and get back to doing the greater works. Some don't like to talk about works. To me, it's a lot like ordering a pizza. As a good Italian, I like my pizza with "the works." In the same way, in the Spirit realm, I love to see the works. I love to see the signs, wonders and miracles. I love the demonstration of the Holy Ghost. I love the demonstration of the power of God. I like to see Him at work in people's lives, transforming them. I want to see them turned upside down and have all of the nonsense shaken out of them.

When the fire of God falls in the power and presence of the Spirit, all of our fleshly attachments fall off. When we come to Him, it is not with our trophies or plaques. No amount of money can buy our way into His presence. No amount of education can qualify us. We stand naked before Him. In that day, all of your fleshly achievements will mean nothing. It will all be burned up as by fire.

Think about John, who became known as the Revelator. When he was banished to the Isle of Patmos, it was a punishment, meant to be a death sentence. Life on that deserted island among many criminals could not have been pleasant. Still, rather than concentrate on the difficulty of his situation, John got in the Spirit on the Lord's Day, and something wonderful began to happen.

John had many reasons to remain in the flesh. He had seen many of his fellow saints killed—beheaded and hung on crosses upside down. He himself had been severely persecuted. It is believed that he was now living in a cave in the company of unscrupulous men, but it was the Lord's day, and he decided to get in the Spirit and out of the flesh.

No sooner had John gotten in the Spirit than he turned and saw the greatest revelation of Jesus Christ ever recorded. Are you looking for a revelation? Then get out of the flesh and into the Spirit. Start weighing what your heart is doing. God Himself is weighing the hearts of men and the hearts of nations. He knows what's flesh and what's Spirit. When His fire falls, only what has been birthed by His Spirit will remain. All else will be consumed.

Again, in John 14, Jesus said:

> *Believe me that I am in the Father, and the Father in me: or else believe me for the very works' sake.* John 14:11

"You may not believe Me for who I am," He was saying, "but can you at least believe My works?" Seeing the works of God will put faith into the hearts of men and women everywhere, life-changing faith! Jesus continued:

The Power to Win

And whatsoever ye shall ask in my name, that will I do, that the Father may be glorified in the Son. John 14:13

We know that Jesus healed the sick and the lame, and He did it to glorify the God of Israel. As we have seen, the result was that He quickly became famous throughout the land—because He cast out demons and healed the sick, and through it all, the name of the God of Israel was glorified! It happened when God's power and presence were released, and we need this same power today.

As a sinner, I didn't understand the Word of God and yet God saved me. As I noted early on, I understood power and knew that I needed it. I needed the power of the Holy Ghost to overcome the life-altering issues and addictions I was facing. Thank God I found that power in His cross, in His resurrection, in His blood that was shed for me, in His name, in His Spirit, in His Word and in His presence.

Now that forty years have gone by, I find that I need His power as much as ever or perhaps even more than ever. This is the power to win, the power to change, the power to overcome, the power to save, the power to heal, the power to deliver, the power to gain wealth. Both the power of God and the presence of God minister to me. I need them both and will not settle for one without the other. Will you join me in contending for *His Light, His Power, His Presence, His Glory*?

Heavenly Father,

I release over all who read this book, the apostolic prayer of Paul from Ephesians 1:17-19:

"That the God of our Lord Jesus Christ, the Father of glory, may give unto you the spirit of wisdom and revelation in the knowledge of him: the eyes of your understanding being enlightened; that ye may know what is the hope of his calling, and what the riches of the glory of his inheritance in the saints, and what is the exceeding greatness of his power to us-ward who believe, according to the working of his mighty power." (KJV)

Now, in closing, I commend to you that, according to this scripture in Habakkuk, you would answer your call and report for duty. And I will see you in the glory.

The Power to Win

For the earth shall be filled with the knowledge of the glory of the Lord, as the waters cover the sea. Habakkuk 2:14

Now is the time for the fulfillment of this great end-time prophetic word by the prophet Habakkuk. It's harvest time. There has been a huge shift in the Spirit. We have hit a turning point, a tipping point, a prophetic *kairos* moment in time!

The Lord is releasing a fresh revelation of His power and His presence, "His glory," to reap and fully enter into harvest glory. Carriers of this revelation will be raised up and launched out with a golden sickle in their hands and fire in their hearts. They have been prepared *"for such a time as this."*

We are about to see an unprecedented move of God that will sweep the nations, with an army anointed for evangelism and with a burden for souls. They will understand that there is an ease in the glory that will carry them to victory. It is *the Power To Win*. It will include a transference of wealth and a release of the very power to gain wealth. Yes, the glory of the latter house will be greater than the former house. It is the greater glory that is to come. This shall come to pass in this generation.

For thus saith the LORD of hosts; Yet once, it is a little while, and I will shake the heavens, and the earth, and the sea, and the dry land; and I will shake all nations, and the desire of all nations shall come: and I will fill this house with glory, saith the LORD of hosts. The silver is mine, and the gold is mine, saith the LORD of hosts. The glory of this latter house shall be greater than of the former, saith the LORD of hosts: and in this place will I give peace, saith the LORD of hosts.

Haggai 2:6-9

May God bless you and your family!

Amen!

NO SOONER HAD JOHN GOTTEN IN THE SPIRIT THAN HE TURNED AND SAW THE GREATEST REVELATION OF JESUS CHRIST EVER RECORDED!

Author Contact Page

You may contact the author in the following ways:

By Email
bro.russ @ eagleworldwide.com

By Phone:
+1 905 308 9991

By Mail:
PO Box 39
Copetown ON L0R1J0
Canada

On Facebook:

facebook.com/eagleworldwide

facebook.com/russ.moyer.52

By visiting his website:
www.EagleWorldwide.com

TRANSFORMATION

Impact

...your Christian Walk

- ► Days of War & Roses
- ► Night Watch
- ► Living on the Prophetic Edge
- ► Razing Hell
- ► Leading on the Prophetic Edge
- ► Can These Bones Live?
- ► Just to Ponder not to Preach

$15
*Each

EAGLE WORLDWIDE
RETREAT & REVIVAL CENTRE

SUMMER CAMP TENT REVIVAL

July through August
8 Powerful Weeks of Revival
Every Night @ 7:00pm

Specialty Schools
School of the Prophets
School of Freedom and Healing
School of the Supernatural

Location: 976 Hwy 52 Copetown ON L0R 1J0
Call for more details 905 308 9991
www.EagleWorldwide.com

WINTER CAMP REVIVAL GLORY

February/March
10 Powerful Days of Revival Glory
Every Night @ 7:00pm

Specialty Schools
School of the Prophets

The Dwelling Place
7895 Pensacola Blvd Pensacola FL 32534
Call for more details 850 473 8255
www.TheDwellingPlaceChurch.org

EAGLE WORLDWIDE NETWORK
CREDENTIALING & SPIRITUALLY COVERING
Ministers
Marketplace Ministers
Traveling & Itinerant Ministers
Missionaries
Churches
Church Networks
Home Churches
Outreach Ministries
And more...
GOVERNING OFFICIAL
PASTOR MAVE MOYER
NETWORK COORDINATOR
PASTOR JOANNA ADAMS
CREDENTIALS AVAILABLE
Certified Practical Minister
Licensed Minister
Ordained Minister
OFFICE@EAGLEWORLDWIDE.COM

INTERNATIONAL COALITION
OF
PROPHETIC
LEADERS

THE INTERNATIONAL COALITION OF PROPHETIC LEADERS is an alliance of fivefold ministers operating in the office gift of the Prophet, from Ephesians 4:11-12, who have chosen to walk in covenant relationship with one another and in alignment with the apostolic movement.

Our primary interest is the restoration of the office gift of the Prophet and the gift of prophecy to the church with character, integrity and proper biblical protocol.

APOSTOLICALLY LED
& PROPHETICALLY
INFLUENCED

ICPLeaders.com

CPSIA information can be obtained
at www.ICGtesting.com
Printed in the USA
LVHW042352110719
623846LV00001B/1

9 781950 398027